knitted
MODERN CLASSICS
for babies

13 beautiful handknit designs

Chrissie Day

QUAIL

KNITTED MODERN CLASSICS FOR BABIES

First published in Great Britain in 2014 by
Quail Publishing
www.quailpublishing.co.uk

Designs: Chrissie Day
Photography: Jesse Wild
Styling: Georgina Brant & Quail Studio
Graphic Design: Quail Studio
Pattern Editing: Jill Gray and Rachel Atkinson

ISBN 978-0-9927707-2-3

Printed in the United Kingdom

INTRODUCTION

Chrissie Day is a widely recognised knitwear designer, tutor and author of nine books covering the world of knitting, crochet and felting. She regularly teaches at venues in the UK and Europe.

This book presents classic, yet modern, items of clothing that can be passed down through family or friends to be treasured. Designs that are reassuringly timeless can be interpreted in the warm pure wools for baby or the cooler wool / cotton mix. Pure fibres are used, allowing a baby's skin to be protected and be able to breathe. Colours can be altered to suit seasons, but the aim of my designing was to recreate the way families used to cherish baby clothes and use them for each new baby member. When the family is complete, you can pack them away ready to clothe those cherished grandchildren in the future.

These items can be knit as gifts and these items will be received with delight at your thoughtfulness. The First Doll is simply a doll safely knit without seams to come undone, and small enough to be held by a young child and treasured.

'My thanks to Darren and all the publishing team at Quail, to Rowan for giving me this opportunity and most of all, my team of knitters. Huge thanks to Nigel, my darling husband, who patiently absorbs all the stress and drama writing a book brings, and also to MJH - you gave me 'tomorrow' and you know who you are.'

'Whilst designing and working on this book my first granddaughter was born and I dedicate this book to her, Abigail, and to all who dream of the babies who will wear these designs.'

Chrissie Day

3

Raglan
Sweater

pg. 30

First Sweater

pg. 34

Christmas
Sweater
pg. 38

Fairisle
Hat

pg. 42

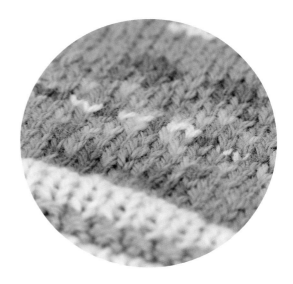

Simple
Bolero
pg. 44

Striped Rompers

pg. 48

Smock
Coat

pg. 52

Baby
Doll

pg. 56

Christmas
Dress
pg. 60

Textured Cardigan

pg. 64

Striped
Coat

pg. 68

Button Cuff
Bootees

pg. 72

PomPom Hat

pg. 74

Raglan
Sweater

Materials

YARN
Rowan Baby Merino Silk DK
A: Lake 696; 2 (2:3:3:3) × 50g balls
B: Aubergine 701; 1 (1:1:1:1) × 50g ball

NEEDLES
Pair of 3.25mm (UK 10/US 3) knitting
needles
Pair of 4mm (UK 8/US 6) knitting needles

EXTRAS
Stitch markers
Stitch holders
12 buttons

MEASUREMENTS

To fit age					
0-3 months	3-6 months	6-9 months	9-12 months	12-18 months	
Actual measurements					
Chest					
52	54	55	57	59	cm
20½	21¼	21½	22½	23	in
Length from back neck					
25	26.5	28	29.5	31	cm
9¾	10½	11	11½	12	in
Sleeve Length					
12	14.5	17	19	21	cm
4¾	5¾	6¾	7½	8¼	in

TENSION
22 sts and 30 rows to 10cm (4in) square over St-st using 4mm needles,
or size to obtain correct tension.

ABBREVIATIONS
See page 78

PATTERN BEGINS
BACK

Using 3.25mm needles and A, cast on 57 (59:61:63:65) sts.

Row 1 (RS): Knit.

This row sets G-st.

Work a further 5 rows in G-st.

Change to 4mm needles and beg with a RS knit row, work in St-st until Back measures 14.5 (15:16.5:17.5:18.5)cm / 5¾ (6:6½:7:7¼)in from cast-on edge, ending with a WS row.

Shape raglan

Placing a marker after the 4th cast-off st, cast off 7 sts at beg of next 2 rows. *43 (45:47:49:51) sts.*

Work 0 (0:2:2:0) rows straight.

Next row (RS): K2, skp, k to last 4 sts, k2tog, k2. *2 sts dec.*

Next row (WS): Purl.

Next row: Knit.

Next row: Purl.

Rep last 4 rows a further 5 (6:6:6:7) times. *31 (31:33:35:35) sts.*

For 1st, 4th and 5th sizes only

Next row: K2, skp, k to last 4 sts, k2tog, k2. *29 (-:-:33:33) sts.*

Next row: Purl.

All sizes again

Place sts on holder and leave to one side.

POCKET LININGS (make 2 alike)

Using 4mm needles and B, cast on 16 sts.

Beg with a RS knit row, work 16 rows in St-st.

Place sts on holder and leave to one side.

FRONT

Using 3.25mm needles and A, cast on 57 (59:61:63:65) sts.

Work 6 rows in G-st as set for Back.

Change to 4mm needles and beg with a RS knit row, work 16 rows in St-st.

Place pocket linings as folls:

Next row (RS): K6 (7:7:8:9), slip next 16 sts to holder and k across 16 sts of first pocket lining, k13 (13:15:15:15), slip next 16 sts to holder and k across 16 sts of second pocket lining, k6 (7:7:8:9). *57 (59:61:63:65) sts.*

Next row (WS): Purl.

Cont in St-st until Front measures 14.5 (15:16.5:17.5:18.5) cm / 5¾ (6:6½:7:7¼)in from cast-on edge, ending with a WS row.

Shape raglan

Cast off 4 sts at beg of next 2 rows. *49 (51:53:55:57) sts.*

Work 0 (0:0:2:0) rows straight.

Next row: K2, skp, k to last 4 sts, k2tog, k2. *2 sts dec.*

Next row: Purl.

Next row: Knit.

Next row: Purl.

Rep last 4 rows a further 4 (4:4:4:5) times. *39 (41:43:45:45) sts.*

For 3rd and 4th sizes only

Next row: K2, skp, k to last 4 sts, k2tog, k2. *- (-:41:43:-) sts.*

Next row: Purl.

All sizes again
Shape neck

Next row (RS): K2, skp, k3 (4:4:5:6), turn and continue on these 6 (7:7:8:9) sts leaving remaining sts on holder.

Work each side of neck separately as folls:

Dec 1 st at neck edge of next 2 (2:2:3:3) rows and **AT THE SAME TIME** dec 1 st at raglan edge as set on foll alt row. *3 (4:4:4:5) sts.*

1st, 2nd and 3rd sizes only

Next row (WS): Purl.

Next row (RS): K1 (2:2:-:-), skp. *2 (3:3:-:-) sts.*

1st size only

Next row (WS): P2tog. Fasten off.

2nd and 3rd sizes only

Next row (WS): Purl.

Next row (RS): K1, skp. *- (2:2:-:-)sts.*

Next row: P2tog. Fasten off.

4th and 5th sizes only
Next row (RS): K2, skp, k- (-:-:-:0:1). - (-:-:-:3:4) sts.
Next row: Purl.
Next row: K- (-:-:-:1:2), skp. - (-:-:-:2:3) sts.

4th size only
Next row (WS): P2tog. Fasten off.

5th size only
Next row (WS): Purl.
Next row (RS): K1, skp. - (-:-:-:-:2) sts.
Next row: P2tog. Fasten off.

All sizes again
With RS facing, working on remaining sts, leave centre 25 sts on a holder, rejoin yarn A and k to last 4 sts, k2tog, k2.
6 (7:7:8:9) sts.
Dec 1 st at raglan edge as set on foll alt row and
AT THE SAME TIME dec 1 st at neck edge of next 2 (2:2:3:3) rows. *3 (4:4:4:5) sts.*

1st, 2nd and 3rd sizes only
Next row (WS): Purl.
Next row (RS): K2tog, k1 (2:2:-:-). *2 (3:3:-:-) sts.*

1st size only
Next row (WS): P2tog. Fasten off.

2nd and 3rd sizes only
Next row (WS): Purl.
Next row (RS): K2tog, k1. - (2:2:-:-) sts.
Next row: P2tog. Fasten off.

4th and 5th sizes only
Next row (RS): K- (-:-:-:0:1), k2tog, k2. - (-:-:-:3:4) sts.
Next row (WS): Purl.
Next row: K2tog, k- (-:-:-:1:2). - (-:-:-:2:3) sts.

4th size only
Next row: P2tog. Fasten off.

5th size only
Next row: Purl.
Next row: K2tog, k1. - (-:-:-:-:2) sts.
Next row: P2tog. Fasten off.

SLEEVES (make 2 alike)
Using 3.25mm needles and A, cast on 27 (29:29:31:31) sts.
Work 6 rows in G-st as set for Back and **AT THE SAME TIME** inc 2 sts evenly across last row. *29 (31:31:33:33) sts.*

Change to 4mm needles and beg with a RS knit row, work in St-st as folls:
Work 2 rows in A.
Work 2 rows in B.
Break B and continue in A only.
Inc row: K1, M1, k to last st, M1, k1. *2 sts inc.*
Work 1 row.
Rep last 2 rows a further 5 (5:4:2:1) times then inc row only once more. *43 (45:43:41:39) sts.*
Work 3 rows.
Inc row: K1, M1, k to last st, M1, k1. *2 sts inc.*
Rep last 4 rows a further 1 (2:4:6:8) times.
47 (51:53:55:57) sts.
Work straight in St-st until Sleeve measures 12 (14.5:17:19:21)cm / 4¾ (5¾:6¾:7½:8¼)in from cast-on edge, ending with a WS row.

Shape raglan
Cast off 4 sts at beg of next 2 rows. *39 (43:45:47:49) sts.*
Place a marker at one end of last row; For Left Sleeve, place marker at beg of row, and for Right Sleeve, place marker at end of row.
Next row (RS): K2, skp, k to last 4 sts, k2tog, k2.
2 sts dec.
Next row: P2, p2tog, p to last 4 sts, p2togtbl, p2. *2 sts dec.*
Rep last 2 rows a further 2 (3:3:3:3) times.
27 (27:29:31:33) sts.
Next row: K2, skp, k to last 4 sts, k2tog, k2. *2 sts dec.*
Next row: Purl.
Rep last 2 rows a further 9 (9:10:11:12) times. *7 sts.*
Leave remaining sts on holder.

SLEEVE BUTTON BORDERS (Both alike)

Join back raglan seams. With RS facing, using 3.25mm needles and A, pick up and k24 (26:28:30:32) sts evenly along front raglan edge of sleeve between marker near underarm and top of back neckband.

Work 6 rows in G-st as set for Back.

Cast off knitwise.

BACK NECKBAND

With RS facing, using 3.25mm needles and A, pick up and k4 sts evenly across button border, k across 7 sts from holder at top of right sleeve, 29 (31:31:33:33) sts from holder at back neck, 7 sts from holder at top of left sleeve and pick up and k4 sts evenly across button border. *51 (53:53:55:55) sts.*

Work 6 rows in G-st as set for Back.

Cast off knitwise.

LEFT FRONT BUTTONHOLE BORDER

With RS facing, using 3.25mm needles and A, pick up and k24 (27:28:31:32) sts evenly up left front raglan edge from inner edge of cast-off sts near underarm.

Work 2 rows in G-st as set for Back.

Next row (WS): K3 (3:4:4:4), k2tog, yf, [k2 (3:3:4:4), k2tog, yf] 3 times, k7 (7:7:7:8).

Work a further 3 rows in G-st.

Cast off knitwise.

RIGHT FRONT BUTTONHOLE BORDER

With RS facing, using 3.25mm (US 3) needles and A, pick up and k24 (27:28:31:32) sts evenly down right front raglan edge to inner edge of cast-off sts near underarm.

Work 2 rows in G-st as set for Back.

Next row (WS)(Buttonhole): K6 (6:6:6:7), k2tog, yf, [k2 (3:3:4:4), k2tog, yf] 3 times, k4 (4:5:5:5).

Work 3 rows in G-st.

Cast off knitwise.

FRONT NECKBAND

With RS facing, using 3.25mm needles and A, pick up and k4 sts evenly across left buttonhole border, 5 (7:7:7:9) sts evenly down left side of neck, k25 sts from holder at front neck, pick up and k5 (7:7:7:9) sts evenly up right side of neck and 4 sts evenly across right buttonhole border.

43 (47:47:47:51) sts.

Work 2 rows in G-st as set for Back.

Next row (WS)(Buttonhole): K3, k2tog, yf, k to last 5 sts, yf, k2tog, k3.

Work 3 rows in G-st.

Cast off knitwise.

POCKET BORDERS (Both alike)

With RS facing, using 3.25mm needles and A, k across remaining 16 sts on holder.

Work 6 rows in G-st as set for Back.

Cast off using the 3-st i-cord method. See page 76.

MAKING UP

Sew row-end edge of front buttonhole border to cast-off sts at underarm, matching cast-off edge to marker. Join front raglan armhole edges along the 4 cast-off sts at underarm. Lay buttonhole borders over button borders and sew row-end edges of button borders in place on inside. Join side and sleeve seams. Sew pocket linings and borders in position. Sew on buttons.

First Sweater

Materials

YARN

Rowan Baby Merino Silk DK

A: Teal 677; 2 (2:2:3:3) × 50g balls

B: Rose 678; 1 (1:1:1:1) × 50g balls

NEEDLES

Pair of 3.25mm (UK 10/US 3) knitting needles

Pair of 4mm (UK 8/US 6) knitting needles

EXTRAS

Locking stitch markers

Stitch holders

3 buttons

MEASUREMENTS

To fit age					
0-3 months	3-6 months	6-9 months	9-12 months	12-18 months	
Actual measurements					
Chest					
51	53	55	57	59	cm
20	21	21½	22½	23	in
Length from back neck					
24.5	26	27.5	29	30	cm
9½	10¼	10¾	11	11½	12	in
Sleeve Length					
12	14.5	17	19	21	cm
4¾	5¾	6¾	7½	8¼	in

TENSION

22 sts and 30 rows to 10cm (4in) over St-st using 4mm needles, or size to obtain correct tension.

ABBREVIATIONS

See page 78

PATTERN NOTES

This sweater is constructed in one piece starting at the bottom Front edge and working upwards, casting on and shaping the sleeves over and into the Back then casting off at the bottom edge.

PATTERN BEGINS
FRONT, BACK AND SLEEVES

Using 3.25mm needles and A, cast on 57 (59:61:63:65) sts.

Row 1 (RS): K1 [p1, k1] to end.

This row sets moss st.

Work a further 2 rows in moss st.

Join in B and work 3 rows in moss st.

Place a marker at each end of last row worked. Break B and continue in A.

Change to 4mm needles.

Starting with a RS knit row, work in St-st until Front measures 12.5 (13.5:14.5:15.5:16.5)cm / 5 (5¼:5¾:6:6½)in from marker, ending with a WS row.

Shape sleeves

Cast on 5 (6:6:6:5) sts at end of next 4 (4:6:6:4) rows. *77 (83:97:99:85) sts.*

Cast on 4 (5:5:6:6) sts at end of next 8 (8:8:8:12) rows. *109 (123:137:147:157) sts.*

Continue as folls:

Row 1 (RS): [K1, p1] 4 times, k to last 8 sts, [p1, k1] 4 times.

Row 2 (WS): [K1, p1] 4 times, k1, p to last 9 sts, k1, [p1, k1] 4 times.

These 2 rows set patt.

Continue straight in patt until Sleeve measures 2.5 (2.5:2.5:3:2.5)cm / 1 (1:1:1¼:1)in, from last cast on, ending with a WS row.

Shape left front neck

Next row (RS): Patt 43 (50:57:62:67) sts, turn and leave remaining sts on holder.

Work each side of neck separately as folls:

Next row (WS): Patt.

Next row: Patt to last 4 sts, k2tog, k2. *42 (49:56:61:66) sts.*

Last 2 rows set neck shaping.

Dec 1 st as set at neck edge of 2nd and 0 (0:1:1:1) foll alt rows. *41(48:54:59:64) sts.*

Continue straight until work measures 6 (6.5:6.5:7:7)cm / 2¼ (2½:2½:2¾:2¾)in from last cast on sts, ending with a WS row.

Shape left back neck

Next row (RS): Patt.

Next row (WS): Kfb, patt to end. *1 st inc.*

Next row: Patt to last st, kfb. *1 st inc.*

Next row: Kfb, patt to end. *44 (51:57:62:67) sts.*

Next row: Patt to end, cast on 8 sts. *52 (59:65:70:75) sts.*

Cont straight until work measures 4cm / 1½in, from last cast on sts, ending with a RS row.

Leave sts on holder.

Shape right front neck

With RS facing, rejoin A to remaining 66 (73:80:85:90) sts, cast off centre 23 sts using the 3-st i-cord method (see page 76), patt to end. *43 (50:57:62:67) sts.*

Next row (WS): Patt.

Next row (RS): K2, skp, patt to end. *1 st dec.*

Last 2 rows set neck shaping.

Dec 1 st as set at neck edge of next RS row and 0 (0:1:1:1) foll alt rows. *41 (48:54:59:64) sts.*

Continue straight until work measures 6(6.5:6.5:7:7)cm / 2¼ (2½:2½:2¾:2¾)in, from last cast on sts, ending with a WS row.

Shape right back neck

Next row (RS): Patt.

Next row (WS): Patt to last st, kfb. *1 st inc.*

Next row: Kfb, patt to end. *1 st inc.*

Next row: Patt to last st, kfb. *44 (51:57:62:67) sts.*

Next row: Patt.

Next row: Patt to end, cast on 8 sts. *52 (59:65:70:75) sts.*

Cont straight until work measures 4cm / 1½in, from last cast on sts, ending with a RS row.

Next row (WS): Patt 52 (59:65:70:75) sts, cast on 5 (5:7:7:7) sts, patt across sts from holder. *109 (123:137:147:157) sts.*

Cont straight until work measures 6 (6.5:6.5:7:7)cm / 2½ (2½:2½:2¾:2¾)in from start of right back neck shaping, ending with a WS row.

Shape sleeves

Cast off 4 (5:5:6:6) sts at end of next 8 (8:8:8:12) rows. *77 (83:97:99:85) sts.*

Cast off 5 (6:6:6:5) sts at end of next 4 (4:6:6:4) rows.

57 (59:61:63:65) sts.

Cont straight in St-st until Back measures 12.5
(13.5:14.5:15.5:16.5)cm / 5 (5¼:5¾:6:6½)in from last cast
off sts, ending with a WS row.

Break A and, change to 3.25mm (US 3) needles and join B.

Work 3 rows in moss st as set for Front.

Break B and rejoin A.

Work a further 3 rows in moss st as set.

Cast off in moss st.

BUTTONHOLE BAND

With RS facing, using 3.25mm needles and A, pick up and
k13 sts down right side of Back opening.

Work 1 (1:2:2:2) rows in moss st as set on Front.

Buttonhole row: Patt 1 (1:2:2:2), patt2tog, yrn, [patt 2,
patt2tog, yrn) twice, patt 2 (2:1:1:1). *3 buttonholes made.*

Work a further 2 (2:3:3:3) rows in moss st.

Cast off in moss st.

BUTTON BAND

With RS facing, using 3.25mm needles and A, pick up and
k13 sts up left side of back opening.

Work 5 (5:6:6:6) rows in moss st as set on Front.

Cast off in moss st.

MAKING UP

Join side and sleeve seams. Sew on buttons.

Placing buttonhole band over buttonband sew to body along
lower edge.

Christmas Sweater

Materials

YARN

Rowan Wool Cotton 4 ply

A: Paper 486 x 2 (3:3:3) x 50g balls

B: Antique 480 x 1 (1:1:1) x 50g balls

NEEDLES

2.75mm (UK /US 2) circular needle, 60cm (24in) length

3.25mm (UK / US 3) circular needle, 60cm (24in) length

Set of 2.75mm (UK /US 2) double-pointed needles

Set of 3.25mm (UK / US 3) double-pointed needles

EXTRAS

Stitch marker

Stitch holders

MEASUREMENTS

To fit age				
0-3 months	3-6 months	6-9 months	9-12 months	
Actual measurements				
Chest				
51	53	55	58	cm
20	21	21½	23	in
Length from back neck				
25.5	27	28.5	30	cm
10	10½	11¼	11¾	in
Sleeve Seam Length				
12	14.5	17	19	cm
4¾	5¾	6¾	7½	in

TENSION

28 sts and 36 rows to 10cm (4in) over St-st using 3.25mm needles, or size to obtain correct tension.

ABBREVIATIONS

See page 78

PATTERN BEGINS

BODY (Worked in the round to the armholes)

Using 2.75mm circular needle and A, cast on 144 (148:156:160) sts. Join to work in the round taking care not to twist sts and place a marker to denote beg of round.

Round 1: [K2, p2] to end.

This round sets 2x2 rib.

Work a further 7 rounds in 2x2 rib and **AT THE SAME TIME** for 2nd and 4th only, inc 2 sts evenly over the last round. *144 (150:156:162) sts.*

Change to 3.25mm circular needle and work St-st in the round (knit every round), until work measures 5.5 (6.5:7.5:8.5)cm / 2 (2½:3:3½)in from cast-on edge.

Commence chart

Join B and continuing to work St-st in the round, commence chart, reading from right to left for every row and working the 24 (25:26:27) st rep 6 times across the round.

Work all 17 rounds of the chart once.

Break B and using A only, work St-st in the round until work measures 15 (16:17:18)cm / 6 (6¼:6½:7)in from cast-on edge.

Divide for front and back

Row 1 (RS): Cast off 4 sts (1 st remains on needle from cast off), k67 (70:73:76), turn. *68 (71:74:77) sts.*

Now work St-st in rows and continue on Front sts only leaving remaining 72 (75:78:81) sts for Back on holder:

Row 2 (WS): Cast off 4 sts, p to end. *64 (67:70:73) sts.*

Shape armholes

Dec 1 st at each end of next 2 (3:3:3) rows, then on 0 (0:1:1) foll alt rows. *60 (61:62:65) sts.*

Work 0 (1:1:3) rows straight.

Shape front neck

Next row (RS): K23 (23:23:24), turn and leave remaining 37 (38:39:41) sts on holder.

Work each side of neck separately as folls:

**Dec 1 st at neck edge on 2nd row then on 6 foll alt rows. *16 (16:16:17) sts.*

Dec 1 st at neck edge on 2nd row then on 2 foll 4th rows.

13 (13:13:14) sts.**

Cont straight until armhole measures 10.5 (12:11.5:12)cm / 4 (4¼:4½:4¾)in, ending with a WS row.

Cast off.

With RS facing, working on remaining 37 (38:39:41) sts from holder, rejoin A, cast off 14 (15:16:17) sts, k to end.

23 (23:23:24) sts.

Work from ** to ** as given for first side of neck.

Continue straight until armhole measures 10.5 (12:11.5:12) cm / 4 (4¼:4½:4¾)in ending with a RS row.

Cast off.

BACK

With WS facing, rejoin yarn to remaining 72 (75:78:81) sts. Cast off 4 sts at beg of next 2 rows. *64 (67:70:73) sts.*

Shape armholes

Dec 1 st at each end of next 2 (3:3:3) rows, then on 0 (0:1:1) foll alt rows.

60(61:62:65) sts.

Continue straight until armhole is 4 rows less than front armhole to shoulder, ending with a WS row.

Shape back neck

Next row (RS): K19 (19:19:20), turn and leave remaining 41 (42:43:45) sts on a holder.

Work each side of neck separately as folls:

Next row (WS): Cast off 3 sts, p to end.

16 (16:16:17) sts.

Next row: Knit.

Next row: Cast off 3 sts, p to end. *13 (13:13:14) sts.*

Cast off remaining 13 (13:13:14) sts.

With RS facing, working on remaining 41 (42:43:45)sts, cast off 22 (23:24:25) sts, rejoin A and k to end.

19 (19:19:20) sts.

Next row: Purl.

Next row: Cast off 3 sts, k to end. *16 (16:16:17) sts.*

Next row: Purl.

Next row: Cast off 3 sts, k to end. *13 (13:13:14) sts.*

Cast off remaining 13 (13:13:14) sts.

SLEEVES

Using 2.75mm DPNs and A, cast on 32 (36:36:40) sts.
Join to work in the round taking care not to twist sts and place a marker to denote beg of round.
Work 8 rounds in 2x2 rib as set on Body and **AT THE SAME TIME** inc 4 sts evenly across last round.
36 (40:40:44) sts.

Change to 3.25mm DPNs and work St-st in the round for 4 rounds.
Inc round: K1, M1, k to last st, M1, k1. *2 sts inc.*
Work 1 (1:1:3) rounds.
Rep last 2 (2:2:4) rounds a further 7 (4:2:7) times then inc round only once more. *54 (52:48:62) sts.*
Work 3 (3:3:5) rounds.
Inc round: K1, M1, k to last st, M1, k1. *2 sts inc.*
Rep last 4 (4:4:6) rounds 1 (4:7:1) times more.
58 (62:64:66) sts.
Work straight until sleeve measures 12 (14.5:17:19)cm / 4¾ (5¾:6¾:7½)in from cast-on edge.

Shape sleeve top

Row 1 (RS): Cast off 4 sts, k to end, turn.
Continue working St-st in rows and cast off 4 sts at beg of next row. *50 (54:56:58) sts.*
Dec 1 st at each end of next 3 (5:5:5) rows, then on 9 (9:10:11) foll alt rows and on foll 3(3:3:3) rows. *20 sts.*
Cast off 3 sts at beg of next 2 rows. *14 sts.*
Cast off remaining 14 sts.

COLLAR

Using 2.75mm circular needle and A, cast on 100 (104:104:108) sts.
Row 1 (RS): P1, [k2, p2] to last 3 sts, k2, p1.
Row 2 (WS): K1, p2, [k2, p2] to last st, k1.
Last 2 rows set rib.
Continue in rib until collar measures 4 (4:5:5)cm / 1½ (1½:2:2)in, ending with row 1.
Next row (WS): Rib 29, pfb, p1, [k2, pfb, p1] 10 (11:11:12) times, rib 29. *111 (116:116:121) sts.*
Next Row: P1, [k2, p2] 7 times, [k3, p2] 10 (11:11:12) times, k3, [p2, k2] 7 times, p1.
Next Row: K1, [p2, k2] 7 times, p3, [k2, p3] 10 (11:11:12)

times, [k2, p2] 7 times, k1.
Cast off in patt.

MAKING UP

Join shoulder seams. Set in sleeves. Sew cast on sts of collar evenly in position all round neck edge. Placing collar left over right, sew evenly in position to cast off sts at front of neck.

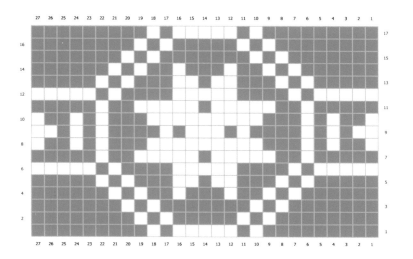

Fairisle Hat

Materials

YARN

Rowan Wool Cotton 4 ply
A: Antique 480; 1 x 50g ball

Rowan Pure Wool 4 ply
1 x 50g ball in each of the following:
B: Shale 402
C: Framboise 456
D: Raspberry 428
E: Gerbera 454

NEEDLES

3.25mm (UK 10/US 3) circular needle,
40cm (16in) length
1 extra needle in a similar size to work the
3-needle cast off

EXTRAS

1 stitch marker
Tapestry needle

MEASUREMENTS

To fit age					
	0-6 months	6-9 months	9-12 months	12-18 months	
Actual measurements					
Circumference					
	34	35	37	39	cm
	13½	13¾	14¼	15	in

TENSION

28 sts and 36 rows to 10cm (4in) over St-st using 3.25mm (US 3)
needle, or size to obtain correct tension.

ABBREVIATIONS

See page 78

PATTERN BEGINS

Using A, cast on 94 (100:104:110) sts.

Join to work in the round, being careful not to twist and place marker for beg of round.

Round 1: [K1, p1] to end.

Rep last round a further 7 times.

Round 9: Using B, knit.

Round 10: Using B, purl.

Round 11: Using A, [K1, p1] to end.

Rep last round a further 3 times.

Round 15: Using B, knit.

For 1st, 3rd and 4th sizes only

Next round: Using B, k6 (-:7:8), [kfb, k15 (-:6:13)] 5 (-:13:7) times, kfb, k to end. *100 (100:118:118) sts.*

All sizes again

Commence chart, reading right to left for every row and changing colours as indicated. Work the 22 rounds working the 20-st rep 5 (5:6:6) times across each round.

Using B only, knit every round until work measures 14 (15:16:16)cm / 5½ (6:6¼:6¼)in from cast-on edge.

Next round: K25 (25:30:30) sts, turn your work inside out, align the tips of the needles parallel to each other and cast off using the 3-needle technique.

Lightly press.

Tassel (Make 2)

Cut 15cm (6in) strands of yarn, 3-4 strands for each colour used, fold in half and secure by wrapping a length of A around and tying to secure.

Insert these ends into tapestry needle and secure at the corner of the hat on the cast off seam inside.

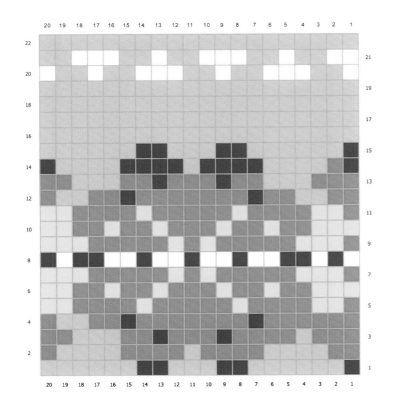

Key

Raspberry

Framboise

Shale

Gerbera

Antique

RS: knit
WS: purl

Materials

YARN

Rowan Pure Wool 4 ply

2(2:3:3:3) x 50g balls in Shell 468

(also shown in Wool Cotton 4ply Prune 506)

NEEDLES

Pair of 2.75mm (UK 12/US 2) knitting needles

Pair of 3.25mm (UK 10/US 3) knitting needles

2.75mm (UK 12/US 2) circular needle, minimum 80cm (32in) length

EXTRAS

2 stitch holders

MEASUREMENTS

To fit age					
0-3 months	3-6 months	6-9 months	9-12 months	12-18 months	
Actual measurements					
Chest					
51	53	55	57	59	cm
20	21	21½	22½	23¼	in
Length from back neck (approx)					
24.5	26	27.5	29	30.5	cm
9½	10¼	10¾	11½	12	in
Sleeve Length					
10	11.5	13	15	17	cm
4	4½	5	6	6¾	in

TENSION

28 sts and 36 rows to 10cm (4in) square over St-st using 3.25mm needles, or size to obtain correct tension.

ABBREVIATIONS

See page 78

PATTERN BEGINS
LEFT FRONT

Using 3.25mm needles, cast on 10 (10:11:12:12) sts.
Row 1 (RS): K to end, cast on 2 sts. *2 sts inc.*
Row 2 (WS): P1, M1, p to end. *1 st inc.*
Rep last 2 rows twice more. *19 (19:20:21:21) sts.*
Row 7: K to last st, M1, k1. *1 st inc.*
Row 8: P1, M1, p to end. *1 st inc.*
Rep last 2 rows a further 3 times. *27 (27:28:29:29) sts.*
Row 15: K to last st, M1, k1. *1 st inc.*
Row 16: Purl.
Rep last 2 rows a further 5 (7:7:7:9) times.
33 (35:36:37:39) sts.
Beg with a RS knit row, work 8 (8:8:10:10) rows straight in St-st.

Shape armhole

Next row (RS): Cast off 3 (4:4:4:5) sts, k to end.
30 (31:32:33:34) sts.
Next row (WS): Purl.
Next row: K1, skp, k to end. *1 st dec.*
Next row: Purl.
Rep last 2 rows twice more. *27 (28:29:30:31) sts.*
Work 4 (4:6:8:4) rows straight in St-st.

Shape front neck

Next row (RS): K to last 4 sts, k2tog, k2. *1 st dec.*
Next row (WS): P2, p2tog, p to end. *1 st dec.*
Rep last 2 rows a further 4 (4:4:5:5) times.
17 (18:19:18:19) sts.
Next row: K to last 4 sts, k2tog, k2. *1 st dec.*
Next row: Purl.
Rep last 2 rows a further 4 (5:5:4:4) times.
12 (12:13:13:14) sts.
Work 6 (6:6:6:8) rows straight in St-st.
Place sts on a holder and leave to one side.

RIGHT FRONT

Using 3.25mm needles, cast on 10 (10:11:12:12) sts.
Row 1 (RS): K1, M1, k to end. *1 st inc.*
Row 2 (WS): P to end, cast on 2 sts. *2 sts inc.*
Rep last 2 rows twice more. *19 (19:20:21:21) sts.*
Row 7: K1, M1, k to end. *1 st inc.*

Row 8: P to last st, M1, p1. *1 st inc.*
Rep last 2 rows a further 3 times. *27 (27:28:29:29) sts.*
Row 15: K1, M1, k to end. *1 st inc.*
Row 16: Purl.
Rep last 2 rows a further 5 (7:7:7:9) times.
33 (35:36:37:39) sts.
Work 9 (9:9:11:11) rows straight in St-st.

Shape armhole

Next row (WS): Cast off 3 (4:4:4:5) sts, p to end.
30 (31:32:33:34) sts.
Next row (RS): K to last 3 sts, k2tog, k1. *1 st dec.*
Next row: Purl.
Rep last 2 rows twice more. *27 (28:29:30:31) sts.*
Beg with a RS knit row, work 4 (4:6:8:4) rows straight in St-st.

Shape front neck

Next row (RS): K2, skp, k to end. *1 st dec.*
Next row (WS): P to last 4 sts, p2togtbl, p2. *1 st dec.*
Rep last 2 rows a further 4 (4:4:5:5) times more.
17 (18:19:18:19) sts.
Next row K2, skp, k to end. *1 st dec.*
Next row P to end.
Rep last 2 rows a further 4 (5:5:4:4) times.
12 (12:13:13:14) sts.
Work 6 (6:6:6:8) rows straight in St-st.
Place sts on a holder and leave to one side.

BACK

Note: The Back is worked downwards from shoulders as follows:
Next row (RS): With RS facing, k across 12 (12:13:13:14) sts from Left Front holder, cast on 35 (37:37:39:39) sts, k across 12 (12:13:13:14) sts from Right Front holder.
59 (61:63:65:67) sts.
Next row (WS): Purl.
Beg with a RS knit row, work 30 (32:34:36:34) straight in St-st.

Shape armholes

Next row (RS): K1, M1, k to last st, M1, k1. *2 sts inc.*
Next row (WS): Purl.

Rep last 2 rows once more.

Next row: K1, M1, k to last st, M1, k1.

65 (67:69:71:73) sts.

Cast on 3 (4:4:4:5) sts at end of next 2 rows.

71 (75:77:79:83) sts.

Beg with a WS purl row, work 34 (38:38:40:44) rows straight in St-st.

Cast off 4 (4:2:3:3) sts at beg of next 2 (2:2:6:6) rows.

63 (67:73:61:65) sts.

Cast off 5 (5:3:4:4) sts at beg of next 4 (4:4:4:4) rows.

43 (47:61:45:49) sts.

Cast off 6 (6:4:4:4) sts at beg of next 2 (2:4:2:2) rows.

31 (35:45:37:41) sts.

Cast off 7 (7:5:5:5) sts at beg of next 2 (2:4:2:2) rows.

Cast off remaining 17 (21:25:27:31) sts.

SLEEVES

Using 2.75mm needles, cast on 35 (37:37:39:39) sts.

Row 1 (RS): K each st tbl to end.

Last row sets twisted G-st.

Rep last row a further 3 times.

Change to 3.25mm (US 3) needles.

Beg with a RS knit row, continue in St-st as follows:

Work 2 rows.

Inc row: K1, M1, k to last st, M1, k1. *37 (39:39:41:41) sts.*

Work 1 row.

Rep last 2 rows a further 10 (8:8:7:8) times, then work inc row only again. *59 (57:57:57:59) sts.*

2nd, 3rd, 4th and 5th sizes only

Work 3 rows.

Inc row: K1, M1, k to last st, M1, k1. *- (59:59:59:61) sts.*

Rep last 4 rows a further - (1:3:4:5) times.

- (61:65:67:71) sts.

All sizes again

Work straight in St-st until Sleeve measures 10 (11.5:13:15:17)cm / 4 (4½:5:6:6¾)in from cast-on edge, ending with a WS row.

Shape sleeve top

Cast off 3 (4:4:4:5) sts at beg of next 2 rows.

53 (53:57:59:61) sts.

Dec 1 st at **each end** of next 3 rows, then on 9 (11:11:12:13) foll alt rows and on foll 3 (1:3:3:3) rows.

23 sts.

Cast off 4 sts at beg of next 2 rows.

Cast off remaining 15 sts.

BORDER

Using mattress stitch, join shoulder and side seams.

With RS facing, using 2.75mm circular needle and beg at side edge of right front, pick up and k10 (10:11:12:12) sts from cast-on edge of right front, 28 (32:32:32:36) sts up shaped edge, 6 (6:6:8:8) sts up straight edge, 23 (25:25:25:27) sts up neck edge to shoulder, 30 (32:32:34:34) sts from back neck, 23 (25:25:25:27) sts down left front neck, 6 (6:6:8:8) sts down straight edge, 28 (32:32:32:36) sts down shaped edge and 10 (10:11:12:12) sts from cast-on edge of left front, 27 (27:29:29:29) sts down shaped edge of back, 17 (21:25:27:31) sts from cast-off edge of back and 27 (27:29:29:29) sts up shaped edge of back.

235 (253:263:273:289) sts.

Work 4 rows in twisted G-st as set on Sleeves.

Working in short rows, continue as follows:

Next row (WS): Patt 180 (193:202:209:221) sts, w&t.

Next row (RS): Patt 54 (58:58:60:64) sts, w&t.

Next row: Patt 43 (46:46:48:52) sts, w&t.

Continue shaping in this way, working to 11 (12:12:12:12) sts before last wrapped st each time until the following row has been worked: Patt 10 (10:10:12:16), w&t.

Work 2 rows across all sts.

Cast off in twisted garter st.

MAKING UP

Join border and Sleeve seams. Set in Sleeves.

Striped Rompers

Materials

YARN

Rowan Wool Cotton 4 ply

A: 2 (2:2:3:3) x 50g balls in Celanden 482

B: 1 (2:2:2:2) x 50g balls in Sea 492

NEEDLES

Pair of 2.75mm (UK 12/US 2)
knitting needles

Pair of 3.25mm (UK 10/US 3)
knitting needles

3.25mm (UK 10/US 3) circular needle,
40cm (16in) length

Note: If you are comfortable working
back and forth on a circular needle you do
not need the additional straight 3.25mm
needle

EXTRAS

4 stitch markers: 2 red, 1 blue and 1 green

2 stitch holders

2 buttons

MEASUREMENTS

To fit age					
0-3 months	3-6 months	6-9 months	9-12 months	12-18 months	

Actual measurements					
Chest					
51	53	55	57	59	cm
20	21	21½	22½	23	in
Length to top of bib					
36.5	39.5	45	49.5	51.5	cm
14¼	15½	17¾	19½	20¼	in

TENSION

36 sts and 38 rows to 10cm (4in) over patt when slightly stretched
using 3.25mm needles, or size to obtain correct tension.

ABBREVIATIONS

See page 78

STITCH PATTERNS

Stripe Sequence (worked over 22 rows)

4 rows in A.

2 rows in B.

6 rows in A.

4 rows in B.

2 rows in A.

4 rows in B.

These 22 rows form stripe sequence and are repeated throughout.

Slip Stitch Rib pattern (worked **FLAT** over 4 rows)

Row 1 (RS): P2, [k2, p2] to end.

Row 2 (WS): Work sts as they occur; knit the knits and purl the purls.

Row 3: P2, [sl 2 sts pwise wyif, p2] to end.

Row 4: Work sts as they occur; knit the knits and purl the purls.

These 4 rows form rib patt and are repeated throughout along with the 22-row stripe sequence.

PATTERN NOTES

When working main body in the round, omit first and last purl stitch of each row in rib pattern to keep pattern correct as set.

When working any shaping in rib pattern only work the 2 slip stitches at each end of rows 3 and 7 if a full pattern repeat can be completed. If not, work the stitches as a knit stitch.

PATTERN BEGINS
RIGHT LEG

Using 3.25mm needles and A, cast on 82 (82:86:98:102) sts. Working stripe sequence and slip stitch rib patt throughout, starting with row 1, work 8 rows.

Shape Sides

Inc 1 st each end of next and 10 (15:11:5:2) foll alt rows, then on 1 (0:4:10:13) foll 4th row, taking inc sts into patt. *106 (114:118:130:134) sts.*

Work straight for 1 (3:3:7:5) rows, ending with a WS row.

Shape crotch

Cast off 4 (4:4:4:5) sts at beg of next 2 rows. *98 (106:110:120:124) sts.*

Dec 1 st each end of next 3 (3:3:5:5) rows, then on foll 1 (1:1:3:2) alt rows. *90 (98:102:106:110) sts.*

Work 1 row. **

Break yarn and leave sts on holder.

LEFT LEG

Work as for Right Leg to **.

DO NOT BREAK YARN. Leave sts on holder.

Join legs

With RS facing, slip sts of both legs onto circular needle. Commence working in rounds continuing to rep stripe sequence and rib patt as set:

Set-up round: Patt across left leg to last st, place red marker, purl remaining left leg st together with the first st of right leg, patt across right leg sts to last st, place second red marker for new beg of round, purl remaining st together with first 2 sts of the round. *177 (193:201:209:217) sts.*

Next round: Patt 43 (47:49:51:53), place blue marker for left side, patt to next red marker, SM, p2tog, patt until 44 (48:50:52:54) sts are on RH needle from last red marker, place a green marker for right side edge, patt to end of round. *176 (192:200:208:216) sts.*

MAIN BODY

Keeping stripe sequence and rib patt correct, work in rounds until body measures 20 (21:22:23:24)cm / 8 (8¼:8¾:9:9½)in from start of crotch shaping ending on an even row of stripe sequence at centre front red marker for crotch, break yarn.

Divide for front and back bib

With RS facing, rejoin appropriate colour to first st after blue marker and work in rows as folls:

Using 3.25mm needles and keeping patt correct, cast off first 7 sts, patt to green marker, turn. *81 (89:93:97:101) sts.*

** **Next row (WS):** Cast off 7 sts, patt to end. *74 (81:86:90:94) sts.*

Next row (RS): K4, place these sts on holder for left

front edging, patt to last 4 sts, turn, leave these 4 sts on a holder for right front edging. *66 (74:78:82:86) sts.*

For 5th size only
Patt 4 rows.

All sizes again
Next row (WS): Patt2tog, patt to last 2 sts, patt2tog. *2 sts dec.*
Next row (RS): Patt.
Rep last 2 rows until 50 (54:54:58:62) sts remain, ending with a RS row.
Next row: Patt 6 (4:4:2:4), [patt2tog, patt 2] to last 4 (2:2:0:2) sts, patt 4 (2:2:0:2). *40 (42:42:44:48) sts.*
Leave these sts on holder.

Right front and left back bib edge
With RS facing using 2.75mm needles and B, sl 4 sts from holder to needle.
Work in G-st until band, when slightly stretched, fits up side edge of bib, ending with a WS row. Break yarn and place sts on holder.
Sew band in place.

Left front and right back bib edge
With WS facing using 2.75mm needles and B, work as for right front bib edging, ending with a WS row.
DO NOT BREAK YARN. Sew band in place.

Front bib edge
Next row (RS): K across 4 sts on needle for left front bib edge, k across 40 (42:42:44:48) sts on holder for front bib, k across 4 sts for right front bib edge.
48 (50:50:52:56) sts.
Knit 3 rows.
Next row (RS)(Buttonhole): K3, yf, k2tog, k to last 5 sts, k2tog, yf, k3.
Knit 4 rows.
Cast off sts knitwise. **

Back bib
With RS facing using 2.75mm needles, place sts left on holder for back onto needle, rejoin appropriate colour to

first st, cast off 7 sts, patt to end, turn. *81 (89:93:97:101) sts.*
Work as given for front bib from ** to ** omitting buttonhole row.

Right back strap
Using 2.75mm needles and B, with RS of back bib facing and beg at right side top edge of bib, pick up and k7 sts, turn.
Work in G-st until strap measures 16cm / 6¼in, ending with a RS row. Cast off sts knitwise.

Left back strap
Using 2.75mm needles and B, starting 7 sts in from left back side top edge of bib, pick up and k7 sts to side edge.
Work in G-st until strap measures 16cm / 6¼in, ending with a RS row.
Cast off sts knitwise.

MAKING UP
Sew up inner leg and crotch seams. Sew buttons onto edge of strap to correspond to buttonholes on front bib edge.

Smock Coat

Materials

YARN
Rowan Baby Merino Silk DK
Claret 700 x 3 (3:4:4:5) x 50g balls

NEEDLES
Pair of 3.25mm (UK 10/US 3) knitting
needles
Pair of 4mm (UK 8/US 6) knitting needles

EXTRAS
Cable needle
2 stitch holders
2 stitch markers
7 buttons

MEASUREMENTS

To fit age					
0-3 months	3-6 months	6-9 months	9-12 months	12-18 months	
Actual measurements					
Chest					
54	56	58	60	62	cm
21¼	22	23	23½	24½	in
Length from shoulder					
33	35.5	38	39.5	42	cm
13	14	15	15½	16½	in
Sleeve Length					
12	14.5	17	19	21	cm
4¾	5¾	6¾	7½	8¼	in

TENSION
22 sts and 30 rows to 10cm (4in) over St-st using 4mm needles, or size
to obtain correct tension.

ABBREVIATIONS
See page 78

SPECIAL ABBREVIATIONS
W5 (Wrap 5): Slip next 5 sts to cable needle and hold at front of
work, wind yarn 3 times around sts on cable needle in an anti-clockwise
direction, then work the sts from the cable needle as folls: K1, p3, k1.

PATTERN BEGINS
BACK
Using 3.25mm needles, cast on 87 (89:93:95:99) sts.
Row 1 (RS): K1, [p1, k1] to end.
This row sets moss st.
Work a further 5 rows in moss st.
Change to 4mm needles and beg with a RS knit row work in St-st until Back measures 16 (18.5:20:21.5:24)cm / 6¼ (7¼:8:8½:9½)in, from cast-on edge, ending with a WS row.

Cont in smocked patt as folls:
Row 1 (RS): P1 (2:4:1:3), k1, [p3, k1] to last 1 (2:4:1:3) sts, p1 (2:4:1:3).
Row 2 (WS): K1 (2:4:1:3), [p1, k3] to last 2 (3:5:2:4) sts, p1, k1 (2:4:1:3).
Row 3: P1 (2:4:1:3), [k1, p3] 0 (0:0:1:1) times, [W5, p3] to last 6 (7:9:10:12) sts, W5, [p3, k1] 0 (0:0:1:1) times, p1 (2:4:1:3).
Row 4: As row 2.
Rows 5-6: As rows 1-2.
Row 7: P1 (2:4:1:3), [k1, p3] 1 (1:1:0:0) times, [W5, p3] to last 10 (11:13:6:8) sts, W5, [p3, k1] 1 (1:1:0:0) times, p1 (2:4:1:3).
Row 8: As row 2.
Rows 9-10: As rows 1-2.
Rows 3-10 set smocked patt.
Work a further 17 rows in smocked patt, ending with a RS row.
Next row (WS): P2 (3:5:6:5), p2tog, [p1, p2tog] 27 (27:27:27:29) times, p2 (3:5:6:5). *59 (61:65:67:69) sts.*

Work in moss st until Back measures 32 (34.5:37:38.5:41)cm / 12½ (13½:14½:15:16)in, ending with a WS row.

Shape back neck
Continue in moss st as folls:
Next row (RS): Patt 20 (20:22:22:23), turn and leave rem 39 (41:43:45:46) sts on a holder.
Work each side of neck separately.
Next row (WS): Cast off 3 sts, patt to end. *17 (17:19:19:20) sts.*
Next row: Patt.
Next row: Cast off 3 sts, patt to end. *14 (14:16:16:17) sts.*
Cast off remaining 14 (14:16:16:17) sts.

With RS facing, rejoin yarn to remaining 39 (41:43:45:46) sts, cast off 19 (21:21:23:23) sts, patt to end.

20 (20:22:22:23) sts
Next row: Patt.
Next row: Cast off 3 sts, patt to end. *17 (17:19:19:20) sts.*
Next row: Patt.
Next row: Cast off 3 sts, patt to end. *14 (14:16:16:17) sts.*
Cast off remaining 14 (14:16:16:17) sts.

LEFT FRONT
Using 3.25mm needles, cast on 48 (49:51:52:54) sts.
Row 1 (RS): K1, [p1, k1] to last 1 (0:0:1:1) sts, p1 (0:0:1:1).
Row 2 (WS): P1 (0:0:1:1), [k1, p1] to last st, k1.
These 2 rows set moss st.
Work a further 3 rows in moss st.
Row 6: Patt 6 sts, leave these 6 sts on holder, M1, patt to end. *43 (44:46:47:49) sts.*

Change to 4mm needles and beg with a RS knit row, work in St-st until Left Front measures 16 (18.5:20:21.5:24)cm / 6¼ (7¼:8:8½:9½)in, from cast-on edge, ending with a WS row.

Work in smocked patt as folls:
Row 1 (RS): P1 (2:4:1:3), k1, [p3, k1] to last st, p1.
Row 2 (WS): K1, [p1, k3] to last 2 (3:5:2:4) sts, p1, k1 (2:4:1:3).
Row 3: P1 (2:4:1:3), [k1, p3] 0 (0:0:1:1) times, [W5, p3] to last 2 sts, k1, p1.
Row 4: As row 2.
Rows 5-6: As rows 1-2.
Row 7: P1 (2:4:1:3), [k1, p3] 1 (1:1:0:0) times, [W5, p3] to last 6 sts, W5, p1.
Row 8: As row 2.
Rows 9-10: As rows 1-2.
Rows 3-10 set smocked patt.
Work a further 17 rows in smocked patt ending with a RS row.
Next row (WS): P1 (2:2:3:2), p2tog, [p1, p2tog] 13 (13:13:13:14) times, p1 (1:3:3:3). *29 (30:32:33:34) sts.*

Work in moss st as folls:
Row 1 (RS): K1, [p1, k1] to last 0 (1:1:0:0) sts, p0 (1:1:0:0).
Row 2 (WS): P0 (1:1:0:0), [k1, p1] to last st, k1.
These 2 rows set moss st.
Continue in moss-st until Left Front measures 29.5 (31.5:34:35.5:36.5)cm / 11½ (12½:13½:14:14¼)in, ending with a RS row.

Shape neck

Next row (WS): Cast off 9 (9:9:10:10) sts, patt to end. *20 (21:23:23:24) sts.*

Dec 1 st at neck edge of next 5 rows, then on 1 (2:2:2:2) foll alt rows. *14 (14:16:16:17) sts.*

Continue straight until Left Front matches Back to shoulder, ending with a WS row.

Cast off remaining *14 (14:16:16:17) sts.*

RIGHT FRONT

Using 3.25mm needles, cast on 48 (49:51:52:54) sts.

Row 1 (RS): P1 (0:0:1:1), [k1, p1] to last st, k1.

Row 2 (WS): K1, [p1, k1] to last 1 (0:0:1:1) sts, p1 (0:0:1:1).

These 2 rows set moss st.

Work a further 3 rows in moss st.

Row 6: Patt to last 6 sts, M1, turn and place remaining 6 sts on holder. *43 (44:46:47:49) sts.*

Change to 4mm needles and beg with a RS knit row work in St-st until Right Front measures 16 (18.5:20:21.5:24)cm / 6¼ (7¼:8:8½:9½)in, from cast-on edge, ending with a WS row.

Work in smocked patt as folls:

Row 1 (RS): P1, k1, [p3, k1] to last 1 (2:4:1:3) sts, p1 (2:4:1:3).

Row 2 (WS): K1 (2:4:1:3), [p1, k3] to last 2 sts, p1, k1.

Row 3: P1, k1, p3, [W5, p3] to last 6 (7:9:10:12) sts, W5, [p3, k1] 0 (0:0:1:1) times, p1 (2:4:1:3).

Row 4: As row 2.

Rows 5-6: As rows 1-2.

Row 7: P1, [W5, p3] to last 10 (11:13:6:8) sts, W5, [p3, k1] 1 (1:1:0:0) times, p1 (2:4:1:3).

Row 8: As row 2.

Rows 9-10: As rows 1-2.

Rows 3-10 set smocked patt.

Work a further 17 rows in smocked patt ending with a RS row.

Next row (WS): P1 (1:3:3:3), p2tog, [p1, p2tog] 13 (13:13:13:14) times, p1 (2:2:3:2). *29 (30:32:33:34) sts.*

Work in moss st as folls:

Row 1: P0 (1:1:0:0), [k1, p1] to last st, k1.

Row 2: K1, [p1, k1] to last 0 (1:1:0:0) st, p0 (1:1:0:0).

These 2 rows set moss st.

Continue in moss st until Right Front measures 29.5 (31.5:34:35.5:36.5)cm / 11½ (12½:13½:14:14¼)in, ending

with a WS row.

Shape neck

Next row (RS): Cast off 9 (9:9:10:10) sts, patt to end. *20 (21:23:23:24) sts.*

Next row (WS): Patt.

Dec 1 st at neck edge of next 5 rows, then on 1 (2:2:2:2) foll alt rows. *14 (14:16:16:17) sts.*

Continue straight until Right Front matches Back to shoulder, ending with a WS row.

Cast off remaining 14 (14:16:16:17)sts.

SLEEVES (Both alike)

Using 3.25mm needles, cast on 31 (33:33:35:35) sts.

Work 6 rows in moss st as set on Back and **AT THE SAME TIME** inc 2 sts evenly across last row. *33 (35:35:37:37) sts.*

Change to 4mm needles.

Beg with a RS knit row, work in St-st as follows:

Work 2 rows.

Inc row (RS): K1, M1, k to last st, M1, k1. *2 sts inc.*

Work 1 (1:1:3:3) rows.

Rep last 2 (2:2:4:4) rows a further 4 (3:3:6:6) times then inc row only once more. *45 (45:45:53:53) sts.*

For 1st and 4th sizes only

Work 2 rows.

Next row (WS): P7 (-:-:11:-), PM, p2, [pfb, p2] 9 times, pfb, p1, PM, p7 (-:-:11:-). *55 (-:-:63:-) sts.*

For 2nd, 3rd and 5th sizes only

Work - (3:3:-:5) rows.

Inc row (RS): K1, M1, k to last st, M1, k1. *2 sts inc.*

Rep last - (4:4:-:6) rows a further - (1:2:-:0) times. *- (49:51:-:55) sts.*

Work - (2:4:-:2) rows.

Next row (WS): P- (9:10:-:12), PM, p2, [pfb, p2] 9 times, pfb, p1, PM, p-(9:10:-:12). *- (59:61:-:65) sts.*

All sizes again

Work in smocked patt as folls:

Row 1 (RS): K to marker, SM, p2, k1, [p3, k1] 9 times, p2, SM, k to end.

Row 2: P to marker, SM, k2, [p1, k3] 9 times, p1, k2, SM, p to end.

Row 3: K to marker, SM, p2, [W5, p3] 4 times, W5, p2, SM, k to end.

Row 4: As row 2.

Rows 5-6: As rows 1-2.

Row 7: K to marker, SM, p2, k1, p3, [W5, p3] 4 times, k1, p2, SM, k to end.

Row 8: As row 2.

Rows 9-10: As rows 1- 2.

Rows 3-10 set smocked patt.

Continue in smocked patt until Sleeve measures 12 (14.5:17:19:21)cm / 4¾ (5¾:6¾:7½:8¼)in from cast-on edge, ending with a RS row.

Cast off in patt.

BUTTONBAND

With RS facing, using 3.25mm needles, rejoin yarn to 6 sts on Left Front holder and continue as folls:

Row 1 (RS): [P1, k1] 3 times.

Row 2 (WS): [K1, p1] 3 times.

These 2 rows set moss st.

Continue in moss st until band, when slightly stretched, is of sufficient length up front to beg of neck shaping, ending with a WS row.

Break yarn and leave sts on holder.

Sew front border in place.

Mark positions for 7 buttons, the first one 3 (3:4:4:4)cm / 1¼ (1¼:1½:1½:1½)in up from lower edge with the last button positioned in 3rd row of the neckband and 5 remaining buttons spaced evenly between.

BUTTONHOLE BAND

With WS facing, using 3.25mm needles, rejoin yarn to 6 sts on Right Front holder and continue as follows:

Row 1 (WS): [K1, p1] 3 times.

Row 2 (RS): [P1, k1] 3 times.

These 2 rows set moss st.

Continue in moss st until band measures same as buttonband when slightly stretched, ending with a WS row and

AT THE SAME TIME work 6 buttonholes to correspond with markers for the 6 bottom buttons as folls:

Buttonhole row (RS): Patt 2 sts, patt2tog, yrn, patt 2 sts.

DO NOT BREAK YARN. Place sts on holder.

Sew front border in position.

NECKBAND

Join shoulder seams.

With RS facing, using 3.25mm needles, work across 6 buttonhole border sts on holder as foll: moss st 4, patt2tog, pick up and k17 (17:19:21:21) sts up right front neck edge, 6 sts down right back neck edge, 19 (21:21:23:23) sts from back neck, 6 sts up left back neck edge, 17 (17:19:21:21) sts down left front neck edge and work across 6 button border sts on holder as foll: patt2tog, moss st 4. *77 (79:83:89:89) sts.*

Work 2 rows in moss st as set on Back.

Next row (Buttonhole row): Moss st to last 4 sts, yrn, patt2tog, p1, k1.

Work a further 3 rows in moss st.

Collar

Cast off 6 sts in patt at beg of next 2 rows.

65 (67:71:77:77) sts.

Continue in moss st until collar measures 5 (5:6:6:7)cm / 2 (2:2½:2½:2¾)in, from cast off sts, ending with a WS row.

Cast off in patt.

MAKING UP

Place markers 10.5 (11:11.5:12:12.5)cm / 4 (4¼:4½:4¾:5)in down from shoulder seam. Matching centre of sleeve to shoulder seam sew sleeves in position between markers. Join side and sleeve seams. Sew on buttons.

Baby Doll

Materials

YARN
Rowan Wool Cotton 4 ply
1 x 50g ball in each of the following shades:
A: Antique 480
B: Prune 506
C: Violet 490
Note: If you have made the Dress on page 60 you should have enough of shades B and C remaining to make the doll and her dress.

NEEDLES
Pair of 3mm (UK 11/US 2½) knitting needles.
Set of 3.25mm (UK10/US 3) DPNs or 3.25mm short circular needle suitable for working small circumferences in the round

EXTRAS
Stitch marker
Stitch holder
Tapestry needle
Toy stuffing
2 small press-studs for the dress

TENSION
28 sts and 36 rows to 10cm (4in) over St-st using 3.25mm needles, or size to obtain correct tension.

ABBREVIATIONS
See page 78

PATTERN NOTES
The doll is knitted in the round starting with the head and worked upwards from the neck. Stitches are picked up at the neck and worked downwards for the body. The arms and legs are then worked after picking up stitches from the body.
The dress is worked flat and seamed together.

PATTERN BEGINS
HEAD
Using 3.25mm DPNs and A, cast on 22 sts.
Join to work in the round, ensuring stitches are not twisted and place marker for beg of round.
Round 1: Knit.
Round 2: [(K2, M1) twice, (k1, M1) 3 times, k2, M1, k2] twice. *34 sts.*
Round 3: Knit.
Round 4: [(K2, M1) twice, k9, (M1, k2) twice] twice. *42 sts.*
Round 5: Knit.
Round 6: [(K2, M1) twice, k13, (M1, k2) twice] twice. *50 sts.*
Round 7: Knit.

Round 8: [(K2, M1) twice, k17, (M1, k2) twice] twice. *58 sts.*

Knit 6 rounds.

Next Round: [P1, spp, k23, p2tog, p1] twice. *54 sts.*

Next Round: P1, spp, k21, p2tog, p2, ssp, p21, p2tog, p1. *50 sts.*

Next Round: P1, spp, k19, p2tog, p2, ssp, p19, p2tog, p1. *46 sts.*

Next Round: P1, spp, k17, p2tog, p2, ssp, p17, p2tog, p1. *42 sts.*

Next Round: P2, k5, p2, k10, p23.

Next Round: P1, spp, k3, p1, k2, p1, k8, p2tog, p2, ssp, p15, p2tog, p1. *38 sts.*

Next Round: P1, spp, p6, k7, p2tog, p2, ssp, p13, p2tog, p1. *34 sts.*

Next Round: P1, spp, p6, k3, p2, p2tog, p2, ssp, p11, p2tog, p1. *30 sts.*

Next Round: [P1, spp, p9, p2tog, p1] twice. *26 sts.*

Next Round: Purl.

Next Round: [P1, ssp, p7, p2tog, p1] twice. *22 sts.*

Next Round: Purl.

Next Row: [P2tog] 11 times. *11 sts.*

Break yarn leaving a 20cm (8in) tail, thread yarn through remaining sts, pull tight and secure. Ensure you stuff the head from the neck opening before you pick up the body stitches.

BODY

With RS facing, beg halfway across back of head, using 3.25mm DPNs and A, pick up and k15 sts from around neck edge of the head.

Join to work in the round and continue as folls:

Round 1: Knit.

Round 2: K1, [M1, k1] to end. *29 sts.*

Knit 5 rounds.

Round 8: [K7, M1] twice, k1, [M1, k7] twice. *33 sts.*

Knit 5 rounds.

Round 14: K1, M1, k17, M1, k15. *35 sts.*

Knit 3 rounds.

Round 18: K2, M1, k15, M1, k3, M1, k15, M1. *39 sts.*

Knit 1 round.

Round 20: K2, k2tog, k11, k2tog, k4, k2tog, k12, k2tog, k2. *35 sts.*

Knit 3 rounds.

Round 24: K2, k2tog, k9, k2tog, k4, k2tog, k10, k2tog, k2. *31 sts.*

Knit 3 rounds.

Round 28: K1, [k2tog] 15 times. *16 sts.*

Purl 1 round.

Next Round: [K2tog] 8 times. *8 sts.*

Break yarn leaving a 20cm (8in) tail, thread yarn through remaining sts. Stuff body before pulling thread tightly and fastening off.

ARMS (Both alike)

Using 3.25mm DPNs and A, starting one round down from body pick-up point, pick up and k12 sts in a circular shape from side of body, making it approx. 7 rounds deep and 5 sts wide.

Knit 23 rounds.

Next Round: [K2tog] 6 times. *6 sts.*

Knit 1 round.

Break yarn leaving a 20cm (8in) tail, thread yarn through remaining sts, stuff the arm, pull sts tight and secure.

LEGS (Both alike)

With RS facing, using 3.25mm DPNs and A, pick up and k15 sts in a circular shape from lower part of body so the legs are one stitch apart at centre. Make each leg approx. 8 sts wide and deep.

Join to work in the round.

Knit 29 rounds.

Purl 3 rounds.

Next round: [P1, p2tog] 5 times. *10 sts.*

Next round: [P2tog] 5 times. *5 sts.*

Break yarn leaving a 20cm (8in) tail, thread yarn through remaining sts, stuff the leg, pull sts tight and secure.

FACE
Mouth

Using C and the tapestry needle, and referring to the images, working on the ninth round up and 7 sts in from edge, bring needle out at the twelfth stitch in this row. Anchor centre point of mouth on centre st of row 6.

Eyes

Using B and the tapestry needle, stitch eyes 6 rows above

mouth, using 2 sts wide to st over bar tacks, 3-4 bar tacks over the width of 2 sts. Make 3 vertical lines above these as shown.

Bow

Using 3.25mm DPNs and C make an i-cord as folls:

Cast on 2 sts. K2, *without turning work slide these 2 sts to opposite end of needle and bring yarn around back to opposite end of row, pulling it quite tightly, k these 2 sts again; rep from * until tie is 20cm (8in) long.

Cast off and stitch securely into place

DRESS
SKIRT

Using 3mm needles and B, cast on 72 sts. ** Beg with a RS knit row, work 2 rows in St-st.

Next row (RS)(Picot row): K1, [k2tog, yo] to last st, k1.

Next row (WS): Purl.

Next row: Join C, k1, [k1, sl 1 pwise wyif] to last st, k1.

Next row: Join A, p1, [p1, sl 1 pwise wyib] to last st, p1.

Next row: Using B, k1, [k1, sl 1 pwise wyif] to last st, k1.

Next row: Using C, p1, [p1, sl 1 pwise wyib] to last st, p1.

Next row: Using A, k1, [k1, sl 1 pwise wyif] to last st, k1.
**

Break B and C and continue in A only as folls:

Next row: Purl.

Next row: K14, k2tog, k4, skp, k28, k2tog, k4, skp, k14. *68 sts.*

Beg with a WS purl row, work 3 rows in St-st.

Next row: K13, k2tog, k4, skp, k26, k2tog, k4, skp, k13. *64 sts.*

Beg with a WS purl row, work 3 rows in St-st.

Next row: K12, k2tog, k4, skp, k24, k2tog, k4, skp, k12. *60 sts.*

Beg with a WS purl row, work 3 rows in St-st.

Next row: K11, k2tog, k4, skp, k22, k2tog, k4, skp, k11. *56 sts.*

Beg with a WS purl row, work 3 rows in St-st.

Next row: K10, k2tog, k4, skp, k20, k2tog, k4, skp, k10. *52 sts.*

Purl 1 row.

Next row: K9, k2tog, k4, skp, k18, k2tog, k4, skp, k9. *48 sts.*

Beg with a WS purl row, work 5 rows in St-st.

Bodice

Next Row (RS): K9, cast off next 6 sts, k18, cast off next 6 sts, k9. *34 sts.*

Next Row (WS): P9, place next 18 sts on holder for bodice front, p9. *18 sts.*

Working in St-st, dec 1 st at each end of next and foll 4th row. *14 sts.*

Purl 1 row.

Next Row: K3, cast off next 8 sts, k2. *6 sts.*

Next row: P3, turn.

Continue on these 3 sts only and work 4 rows in St-st.

Change to B and beg with a RS knit row, work 4 rows in St-st.

Cast off.

With WS facing, rejoin A to remaining 3 sts and complete to match first side of neck.

Bodice Front

With RS facing, rejoin A to 18 sts from holder.

Row 1 (RS): Skp, k14, k2tog. *16 sts.*

Beg with a WS purl row, work 5 rows in St-st.

Next Row: K4, k2tog, k4, k2tog, k4. *14 sts.*

Next Row: P3, cast off next 8 sts, p2. *8 sts.*

Next row: K3, turn.

Working on these 3 sts only, work 5 rows in St-st.

Cast off.

With WS facing, rejoin A to last 3 sts and complete to match first side of neck.

SLEEVES

Using 3mm needles and B, cast on 24 sts.

Work from ** to ** as given for skirt.

Beg with a WS purl row and working in St-st throughout, continue in stripe sequence as folls:

3 rows in A.

1 row in B.

1 row in C.

3 rows in A.

2 rows in B.

1 row in A.

3 rows in C.

1 row in B.

4 rows in A.

Cast off.

Join sleeve seam and sew sleeve into armhole.

Neck Edging

Front edge

With RS facing, using 3mm needles and C, pick up and k12 sts evenly around front neck edge.

Next Row (WS): Purl.

Cast off.

Back edge

Work as front edge but picking up along back neck edge.

Making up

Fold back sleeve and skirt hem at the picot edging and stitch in place. Join centre at centre back of dress. Stitch a small press-stud to each shoulder tab.

Christmas Dress

Materials

YARN

Rowan Wool Cotton 4 ply

A: 1 (1:1:1:1)x 50g balls in Prune 506
B: 1 (1:1:1:1)x 50g balls in Violet 490
C: 3 (3:3:3:4)x 50g balls in Antique 480

NEEDLES

Pair of 2.75mm (UK 12/US 2) knitting
needles
Pair of 3.25mm (UK 10/US 3) knitting
needles

EXTRAS

Stitch holders
4 buttons

MEASUREMENTS

To fit age					
0-3 months	3-6 months	6-9 months	9-12 months	12-18 months	

Actual measurements					
Chest					
51	54	56	58	60	cm
20	21¼	22	22¾	23½	in
Length from back neck					
42	43.5	45	46.5	48	cm
16½	17	17¾	18¼	19	in
Sleeve Seam Length					
12	14.5	17	19	21	cm
4¾	5¾	6¾	7½	8¼	in

TENSION

28 sts and 36 rows to 10cm (4in) square over St-st using 3.25mm
needles, or size to obtain correct tension.

ABBREVIATIONS

See page 78

PATTERN BEGINS

BACK AND FRONT (Both alike)

Using 2.75mm needles and A, cast on 90(96:100:110:118) sts.

** Beg with a RS knit row, work 2 rows in St-st.

Next row (RS)(Picot row): K1, [k2tog, yf] to last st, k1.

Next row (WS): Purl.

Join in B and work as folls:

Row 1 (RS): Using B, k1, [k1, sl 1 pwise wyif] to last st, k1.

Row 2 (WS): Using C, p1, [p1, sl 1 pwise wyib] to last st, p1.

Row 3: Using A, k1, [k1, sl 1 pwise wyif] to last st, k1.

Row 4: Using B, p1, [p1, sl 1 pwise wyib] to last st, p1.

Row 5: Using C, k1, [k1, sl 1 pwise wyif] to last st, k1.

Row 6: Using A, p1, [p1, sl 1 pwise wyib] to last st, p1.

Rows 7-10: As rows 1-4.

Break off A and B. **

Change to 3.25mm needles.

Using C only, beg with a RS knit row, continue in St-st and work 2 rows.

Dec row: K11, skp, k to last 13 sts, k2tog, k11. *2 sts dec.*

Work 9 (9:9:5:5) rows.

Rep last 10 (10:10:6:6) rows a further 1 (5:9:1:11) times then dec row only a further 0 (0:1:0:0) times.

86 (84:78:106:94) sts.

1st, 2nd, 4th and 5th sizes only

Dec row: K11, skp, k to last 13 sts, k2tog, k11. *2 sts dec.*

Work 11 (11:-:7:7) rows.

Rep last 12 (12:-:8:8) rows a further 5 (2:-:10:3) times then dec row only once again. *72 (76:-:82:84) sts.*

All sizes again

Work straight in St-st until work measures 31 (32:33:34:35) cm / 12 (12½:13:13¼:13¾)in from cast-on edge, ending with a WS row.

Shape armholes

Cast off 3 (3:3:4:4) sts at beg of next 2 rows.

66 (70:72:74:76) sts.

Dec 1 st at each end of next 3 rows, then on 1 (2:2:2:2) foll alt rows. *58 (60:62:64:66) sts.*

Work straight until armhole measures 8 (8:8.5:9:9)cm / 3 (3:3¼:3½:3½)in, ending with a WS row.

Shape neck

Next row (RS): K18 (19:20:20:21), turn and leave remaining 40 (41:42:44:45) sts on a holder.

Work each side of neck separately as folls:

Next row (WS): Cast off 4 sts, p to end.

14 (15:16:16:17) sts.

Next row: Knit.

Dec 1 st at neck edge of next 2 (3:3:3:3) rows.

12 (12:13:13:14) sts.

Work 3 (4:4:4:6) rows straight.

Cast off.

With RS facing, leaving central 22 (22:22:24:24) sts on a holder, rejoin yarn to remaining 18 (19:20:20:21) sts and k to end.

Next row (WS): Purl.

Next row: Cast off 4 sts, k to end. *14 (15:16:16:17) sts.*

Next row: Purl.

Dec 1 st at neck edge of next 2 (3:3:3:3) rows.

12 (12:13:13:14) sts.

Work 2 (3:3:3:5) rows straight.

Cast off.

SLEEVES

Using 2.75mm needles and A, cast on 40 (42:42:44:44) sts.

Work as for Back and Front from ** to **.

Stripe sequence is worked as folls over 14 rows:

3 rows in C.

1 row in A.

1 row in B.

3 rows in C.

2 rows in A.

1 row in C.

2 rows in B.

1 row in A.

Change to 3.25mm needles and beg with a RS knit row, continue in St-st and stripe sequence as folls:

Work 2 rows.

Inc row (RS): K1, M1, k to last st, M1, k1. *2 sts inc.*

Work 1 (1:1:3:3) rows straight.

Rep last 2 (2:2:4:4) rows a further 5 (3:0:6:9) times then inc row only once again. *54 (52:46:60:66) sts.*

Work 3 (3:3:5:5) rows straight.

Inc row (RS): K1, M1, k to last st, M1, k1. *2 sts inc.*

Rep last 4 (4:4:6:6) rows a further 1 (4:8:2:1) times. *58 (62:64:66:70) sts.*

Work straight until Sleeve measures 12 (14.5:17:19:21)cm / 4¾ (5¾:6¾:7½:8¼)in from cast-on edge, ending with a WS row.

Shape sleeve top

Cast off 3 (3:3:4:4) sts at beg of next 2 rows. *52 (56:58:58:62) sts.*

Dec 1 st at each end of next 3 (5:5:3:5) rows then on 9 (9:10:12:12) foll alt rows and on 3 foll rows. *22 sts.*

Cast off 4 sts at beg of next 2 rows. *14 sts.*

Cast off remaining 14 sts.

BACK AND FRONT NECKBANDS (Both alike)

With RS facing, using 2.75mm needles and A, pick up and k12 (14:14:14:16) sts evenly down side of neck, k across 22 (22:22:24:24) sts from holder at back/front neck, pick up and k12 (14:14:14:16) sts evenly up side of neck. *46 (50:50:52:56) sts.*

Row 1 (WS): Using B, p1, [p1, sl 1 pwise wyib], to last st, p1.

Row 2 (RS): Using B, k1, [k1, sl 1 pwise wyif] to last st, k1.

Row 3: Using A, p1, [p1, sl 1 pwise wyib] to last st, p1.

Row 4: Using B, k1, [k1, sl 1 pwise wyif] to last st, k1.

Rows 5-6: As rows 2-3.

Using A, cast off knitwise.

BACK SHOULDER EDGINGS (Both alike)

With RS facing, using 2.75mm needles and A, pick up and k15 (15:16:16:17) sts from shoulder and neckband edge.

Knit 10 rows in G-st.

Cast off.

RIGHT FRONT SHOULDER EDGING

With RS facing, using 2.75mm needles and A, pick up and k15 (15:16:16:17) sts from neckband and shoulder edge.

Knit 4 rows in G-st.

Next row (Buttonhole row): K4 (4:4:4:5), k2tog, yf, k4 (4:5:5:5), k2tog, yf, k3.

Knit 5 rows in G-st.

Cast off.

LEFT FRONT SHOULDER EDGING

With RS facing, using 2.75mm needles and A, pick up and k15 (15:16:16:17) sts from shoulder and neckband edge.

Knit 4 rows in G-st.

Next row (Buttonhole row): K3, yf, k2tog, k4 (4:5:5:5), yf, k2tog, k4 (4:4:4:5).

Knit 5 rows in G-st.

Cast off.

MAKING UP

Lay front shoulder edgings over back shoulder edgings and sew row-end

edges of shoulder edgings in place on side edge. Join side and sleeve seams. Set in sleeves. Fold first 2 rows of body and sleeves onto WS and slip stitch in position to form picot hems. Sew on buttons.

Textured Cardigan

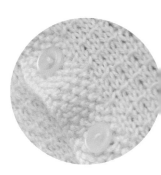

Materials

YARN

Rowan Baby Merino Silk DK

Snowdrop 670; 3(3:3:3)x50g balls

NEEDLES

Pair of 3.25mm (UK 10/US 3) knitting
needles

Pair of 4mm (UK 8/US 6) knitting needles

EXTRAS

Stitch holders

6 buttons

MEASUREMENTS

To fit age				
3-6 months	6-9 months	9-12 months	12-18 months	

Actual measurements				
Chest				
55	57	59	62	cm
21½	22½	23	24½	in
Length from shoulder				
26.5	27.5	29.5	31	cm
10½	11	11½	12	in
Sleeve Length				
14.5	17	19	21	cm
5¾	6¾	7½	8¼	in

TENSION

24 sts and 40 rows to 10cm (4in) square over dimple patt using 4mm
needles, or size to obtain correct tension.

ABBREVIATIONS

See page 78

SPECIAL ABBREVIATIONS

slp   Slip 1 stitch purlwise;

PATTERN BEGINS
BACK
Using 3.25mm needles, cast on 67(69:71:75) sts.

Row 1 (RS):K1, [p1, k1] to end.

This row sets moss st.

Work a further 7(7:9:9) rows in moss st.

Change to 4mm needles.

Continue in dimple patt as folls:

Row 1 (RS): K1(2:1:1), [slp wyif, k1] to last 0(1:0:0) st, k0(1:0:0).

Row 2 (WS): P0(1:0:0), [p1, slp wyib] to last 1(2:1:1) sts, p1(2:1:1).

Row 3: Knit.

Row 4: Purl.

Row 5: K1(2:1:1), [k1, slp wyif] to last 2(3:2:2) sts, k2(3:2:2).

Row 6: P2(3:2:2), [slp wyib, p1] to last 1(2:1:1)sts, p1(2:1:1).

Row 7: Knit.

Row 8: Purl.

These 8 rows set pattern.

Work in patt until Back measures 15.5(16:17.5:18.5) cm/6(6¼:7:7¼)in from cast-on edge, ending with a WS row.

Shape armholes
Keeping patt correct throughout, cast off 2(2:2:3) sts at beg of next 2 rows. *63(65:67:69) sts.*

Dec 1 st at each end of next 3 rows, then on 2 foll alt rows. *53(55:57:59) sts.*

Cont straight until armhole measures 10(10.5:11:11.5)cm/4(4:4¼:4½)in, ending with a WS row.

Shape back neck
Next row (RS): K16(16:17:17), turn and leave remainingsts on holder.

Work each side of neck separately as folls:

Next row (WS): Cast off 3 sts, patt to end. *13(13:14:14) sts.*

Next row: Patt to end.

Next row: Cast off 3 sts, patt to end. *10(10:11:11) sts.*

Cast off remaining 10(10:11:11) sts.

With RS facing, rejoin yarn to remaining sts, cast off 21 (23:23:25) sts, patt to end. *16 (16:17:17) sts.*

Next row (WS): Patt to end.

Next row: Cast off 3 sts, patt to end. *13(13:14:14) sts.*

Next row: Patt to end.

Next row: Cast off 3 sts, patt to end. *10(10:11:11) sts.*

Cast off rem 10(10:11:11)sts.

LEFT FRONT
Using 3.25mm needles, cast on 31(32:33:35) sts.

Row 1 (RS):K1, [p1, k1] to last 0(1:0:0) st, p0(1:0:0).

Row 2 (WS): P0(1:0:0), [k1, p1] to last st, k1.

These 2 rows set moss st.

Work a further 6(6:8:8) rows in moss st.

Change to 4mm needles.

Continue in dimple patt as folls:

Row 1 (RS): K1(2:1:1), [slp wyif, k1] to end.

Row 2 (WS):[P1, slp wyib] to last 1(2:1:1) sts, p1(2:1:1).

Row 3: Knit.

Row 4: Purl.

Row 5: K1(2:1:1), [k1, slp wyif] to last 2 sts, k2.

Row 6: P2, [slp wyib, p1] to last 1(2:1:1) sts, p1(2:1:1).

Row 7: Knit.

Row 8: Purl.

These 8 rows set pattern.

Work in patt until Left Front measures 15.5(16:17.5:18.5) cm/6(6¼:7:7¼)in from cast-on edge, ending with a WS row.

Shape armhole
Keeping patt correct throughout work as folls:

Next row (RS): Cast off 2(2:2:3) sts, patt to end. *29(30:31:32) sts.*

Next row (WS): Patt to end.

Dec 1 st at armhole edge of next 3 rows, then on 2 foll alt rows. *24(25:26:27) sts.*

Cont straight until armhole measures 7(7.5:8:8) cm/2¾(3:3¼:3¼)in, ending with a RS row.

Shape neck and shoulder
Next row (WS): Cast off 9(10:10:10) sts, patt to end. *15(15:16:17) sts.*

65

Dec 1 st at neck edge of next 3 rows, then on 2(2:2:3) foll alt rows. *10(10:11:11) sts.*

Cont straight until armhole matches back armhole to beg of shoulder shaping, ending with a WS row.

Cast off rem 10(10:11:11) sts.

RIGHT FRONT

Using 3.25mm needles, cast on 31(32:33:35) sts.

Row 1 (RS): P0(1:0:0), [k1, p1] to last st, k1.

Row 2 (WS): K1, [p1, k1] to last 0 (1:0:0) st, p0(1:0:0).

These 2 rows set moss st.

Work a further 6(6:8:8) rows in moss st.

Change to 4mm (US 6) needles.

Cont in dimple patt as folls:

Row 1 (RS): K1, [s1p wyif, k1] to last 0(1:0:0) st, k0(1:0:0).

Row 2 (WS): P0(1:0:0), [p1,s1p wyib] to last st, p1.

Row 3: Knit.

Row 4: Purl.

Row 5: K2, [k1, s1p wyif] to last 2(3:2:2) sts, k2(3:2:2).

Row 6: P2 (3:2:2), [s1p wyib, p1] to last 2 sts, p2.

Row 7: Knit.

Row 8: Purl.

These 8 rows set dimple pattern.

Work in patt until Right Front measures 15.5(16:17.5:18.5) cm/6(6¼:7:7¼)in from cast-on edge, ending with a RS row.

Shape armhole

Keeping patt correct throughout work as folls:

Next row (WS): Cast off 2(2:2:3) sts, patt to end. *29(30:31:32) sts.*

Dec 1 st at armhole edge of next 3 rows, then on 2 foll alt rows. *24(25:26:27) sts.*

Cont straight until armhole measures 7(7.5:8:8) cm/2¾(3:3¼:3¼)in, ending with a WS row.

Shape neck and shoulder

Next row (RS): Cast off 9(10:10:10) sts, patt to end. *15(15:16:17) sts.*

Next row (WS): Patt to end.

Dec 1 st at neck edge of next 3 rows, then on 2(2:2:3) foll alt rows. *10(10:11:11) sts.*

Cont straight until armhole matches Back armhole to beg of shoulder shaping, ending with a WS row.

Cast off rem 10(10:11:11) sts.

SLEEVES (make 2 alike)

Using 3.25mm needles, cast on 31(33:33:35) sts.

Work 8(8:10:10) rows in moss st as set on Back and **AT THE SAME TIME** inc 2 sts evenly across last row. *33(35:35:37) sts.*

Change to 4mm needles.

Cont in dimple patt as follsworking increased sts in patt:

Row 1 (RS): K1, [s1p wyif, k1] to end.

Row 2 (WS): [P1, s1p wyib] to last st, p1.

Row 3: Knit.

Row 4: Purl.

Row 5: K1, M1, [k1, s1p wyif] to last 2 sts, k1, M1, k1. *35(37:37:39) sts.*

Last row sets Sleeve shaping.

Row 6: P1, [s1p wyib, p1] to end.

Row 7: [K1, M1] 1(1:1:0) times, k to last 1 (1:1:0) st, [M1, k1] 1(1:1:0) times. *37(39:39:39) sts.*

Row 8: Purl.

These 8 rows set patt.

1st, 2nd and 3rd sizes only

Next row (RS): Patt 1, M1, patt to last st, M1, patt 1. *39(41:41:-:-) sts.*

Work 1 row in patt.

Rep last 2 rows a further 6(1:0:-:-) times. *51(43:41:-:-) sts.*

All sizes again

Next row (RS): Patt 1, M1, patt to last st, M1, patt 1. *2 sts inc.*

Work 3 rows in patt.

Rep last 4 rows a further 0(5:7:9) times then inc row once more. *55(57:59:61) sts.*

Work straight until Sleeve measures 14.5(17:19:21) cm/5¾(6¾:7½:8¼)in from cast-on edge, ending with a WS row.

Shape sleeve top

Cast off 2(2:2:3) sts at beg of next 2 rows. *51(53:55:55) sts.*

Dec 1 st at each end of next 5 rows, on 9(10:11:13) foll alt
rows, then on foll 5(5:5:3) rows. *13 sts.*
Cast off 3 sts at beg of next 2 rows. *7 sts.*
Cast off rem 7 sts.

NECK EDGE

Join shoulder seams.
With RS facing, using 3.25mm needles, beg at neck shaping,
pick up and k19(21:21:21) sts up right front neck edge,
33(35:35:37) sts from back neck and 19(21:21:21) sts down
left front neck edge to beg of neck shaping. *71(77:77:79) sts.*
Work 8(8:10:10) rows in moss st as set on Back.
Cast off in patt.

BUTTONHOLE BAND

With RS facing, using 3.25mm needles, pick up and
k71(75:81:85) sts up right front edge and neckband.
Work 3 rows in moss st as set on Back.
Buttonhole row (RS): Patt 3 (2:3:2), sl1 wyif, take yarn
back, (leave yarn in back until directed otherwise), [sl1, pass
slipped st over previous slipped st] 3 times (3 sts cast off),
place the last st back on left hand needle, turn and wyibusing
the cable cast on method, cast 3 sts onto left hand needle,
cast on 1 more st but before putting st on left needle bring
yarn between 2 sts and to the front, turn, patt 1, pass final
cast on st over the st you have just worked, patt 1, [patt
7(8:9:10), sl1 wyif, take yarn back, (leave yarn in back until
directed otherwise), [sl1, pass slipped st over previous
slipped st] 3 times (3 sts cast off), place the last st back
on left hand needle, turn and wyib using the cable cast on
method, cast 3 sts onto left hand needle, cast on 1 more st
but before putting st on left needle bring yarn between 2
sts and to the front, turn, patt 1, pass final cast on st over
the st you have just worked, patt 1] to last 3 sts, patt 3. *6
buttonholes made.*
Work a further 4 rows in moss st.
Cast off in moss st.

BUTTON BAND

With RS facing, using 3.25mm needles, pick up and
k71(75:81:85) sts down neckband and left front edge.
Work 8 rows in moss st as set on Back.
Cast off in moss st.

MAKING UP

Join side and sleeve seams. Set in sleeves. Sew on buttons.

Striped Coat

Materials

YARN

Rowan Baby Merino Silk DK

A: 1(2:2:2) x 50g balls in Zinc 681

B: 1(1:1:1) x 50g in Straw 671

C: 1(2:2:2) x 50g in Aubergine 701

Rowan Wool Cotton 4ply

D: 1(1:1:1) x 50g in Prune 506

NEEDLES

Pair of 3.25mm (UK 10/US 3) knitting
needles

Pair of 4mm (UK 8/US 6) knitting needles

EXTRAS

Stitch holders

3 buttons

MEASUREMENTS

To fit age				
3-6 months	6-9 months	9-12 months	12-18 months	

Actual measurements				
Chest				
56	58	60	62	cm
22	23	23½	24½	in
Length from shoulder				
37	38.5	39.5	41.5	cm
14½	15	15½	16¼	in
Sleeve Length				
14.5	17	19	21	cm
5¾	6¾	7½	8¼	in

TENSION

22 sts and 30 rows to 10cm (4in) square over St-st using 4mm needles
and Baby Merino Silk DK, or size to obtain correct tension.

ABBREVIATIONS

See page 78

STITCH PATTERNS

Stripe Sequence (worked over 16 rows)

2 rows in A.

2 rows in B.

2 rows in C.

2 rows in A.

1 row in B.

2 rows in C.

2 rows in A.

1 row in B.

2 rows in C.

These 16 rows set stripe sequence patt.

PATTERN BEGINS

BACK

Using 3.25mm needles and holding two ends of D together, cast on 81 (83:87:89) sts.

Starting with a RS row, working in G-st, knit 6 rows.

Change to 4mm needles and holding one strand of Baby Merino Silk DK, beg with a RS knit row, work in St-st and stripe sequence throughout, work 52 (54:56:60) rows in St-st.

Next row (RS): K1 (2:4:5), k2tog, [k2, k2tog] 19 times, k2 (3:5:6). *61 (63:67:69) sts.*

Work 5 rows straight.

Shape armholes

Keeping stripe sequence correct, cast off 2 (2:3:4) sts at beg of next 2 rows. *57 (59:61:61) sts.*

Working in moss st throughout, dec 1 st at each end of next 3 rows, then on 2 foll alt rows. *47 (49:51:51) sts.*

Work straight until armhole measures 10 (10.5:11:11.5)cm / 4 (4:4¼:4½)in, ending with a WS row.

Shape back neck

Next row (RS): K13 (14:14:14), turn and leave remaining sts on holder.

Work each side of neck separately as folls:

Next row (WS): Cast off 3 sts, p to end.
10 (11:11:11) sts.

Next row: Knit.

Next row: Cast off 3 sts, p to end. *7 (8:8:8) sts.*

Cast off remaining 7 (8:8:8) sts.

With RS facing, rejoin yarn to remaining sts, cast off 21 (21:23:23) sts, patt to end. *13 (14:14:14) sts.*

Next row: Purl.

Next row: Cast off 3 sts, k to end. *10 (11:11:11) sts.*

Next row: Purl.

Next row: Cast off 3 sts, k to end. *7 (8:8:8) sts.*

Cast off remaining 7 (8:8:8) sts.

LEFT FRONT

Using 3.25mm needles and holding two ends of D together, cast on 38 (39:41:42) sts and work 6 rows in G-st as set on Back.

Change to 4mm needles and holding one strand of Baby Merino Silk DK, beg with a RS knit row, work 68 (70:72:76) rows in St-st and stripe sequence throughout as set for Back.

Next row (RS): K2 (3:4:5), [k2tog, k1, k2tog, k2] 5 times, k1 (1:2:2). *28 (29:31:32) sts.*

Work 5 rows straight.

Shape armhole

Keeping stripe sequence correct throughout work as folls:

Next row (RS): Cast off 2 (2:3:4) sts, k to end.
26 (27:28:28) sts.

Next row (WS): Purl.

Next row: K2tog, [p1, k1] to last 2 (1:2:2) sts, p1, k1 (0:1:1). *25 (26:27:27) sts.*

Next row: K1 (0:1:1), p1, [k1, p1] to last 3 (2:3:3) sts, k1 (0:1:1), patt2tog. *24 (25:26:26) sts.*

Last 2 rows set moss st and armhole shaping.

Working in moss st throughout dec 1 st at armhole edge of next row, then on 2 foll alt rows. *21 (22:23:23) sts.*

Continue straight until armhole measures 7 (7.5:8:8)cm / 2¾ (3:3¼:3¼)in, ending with a RS row.

Shape neck and shoulder

Next row (WS): Cast off 9 (9:10:10) sts, patt to end.
12 (13:13:13) sts.

Dec I st at neck edge of next 3 rows, then on 2 foll alt rows. 7 *(8:8:8) sts.*

Continue straight until armhole matches Back armhole to beg of shoulder shaping, ending with a WS row.

Cast off remaining 7 (8:8:8) sts.

RIGHT FRONT

Using 3.25mm needles and holding two ends of D together, cast on 38 (39:41:42) sts and work 6 rows in G-st as set on Back.

Change to 4mm needles and holding one strand of Baby Merino Silk DK, beg with a RS knit row, work 68 (70:72:76) rows in St-st and stripe sequence as set for Back.

Next row (RS): K1 (1:2:2), [k2tog, k1, k2tog, k2] 5 times, k2 (3:4:5). *28 (29:31:32) sts.*

Work 6 rows straight.

Shape armhole

Keeping stripe sequence correct throughout work as folls:

Next row (WS): Cast off 2 (2:3:4) sts, k to end. *26 (27:28:28) sts.*

Next row (RS): K1 (0:1:1), p1, [k1, p1] to last 2 sts, k2tog. *25 (26:27:27) sts.*

Next row: Patt2tog, k1(0:1:1), [p1, k1] to last 2 (1:2:2) sts, p1, k1 (0:1:1). *24 (25:26:26) sts.*

Last 2 rows set moss st and armhole shaping.

Working in moss st throughout dec I st at armhole edge of next row, then on 2 foll alt rows. *21 (22:23:23) sts.*

Continue straight until armhole measures 7 (7.5:8:8)cm / 2¾ (3:3¼:3¼)in, ending with a WS row.

Shape neck and shoulder

Next row (RS): Cast off 9 (9:10:10) sts, patt to end. *12 (13:13:13) sts.*

Next row (WS): Patt to end.

Dec I st at neck edge of next 3 rows, then on 2 foll alt rows. 7 *(8:8:8) sts.*

Continue straight until armhole matches back armhole to beg of shoulder shaping, ending with a WS row.

Cast off remaining 7 (8:8:8) sts.

SLEEVES (make 2 alike)

Using 3.25mm needles and holding two ends of D together, cast on 31 (31:33:33) sts and work 6 rows in G-st as set on Back.

Change to 4mm needles and holding one strand of Baby Merino Silk DK, beg with a RS knit row and 3rd (9th:5th:3rd) row of stripe sequence, working in St-st and stripe sequence as given for Back and work 4 rows.

Next row (RS): K1, M1, k to last st, M1, k1. *2 sts inc.*

Work 3 rows straight.

Rep last 4 rows a further 6 (5:2:1) times then inc row once more. *47(45:41:39) sts.*

For 2nd, 3rd and 4th sizes only

Next row (RS): K1, M1, k to last st, M1, k1. *2 sts inc.*

Work 5 rows straight.

Rep last 6 rows a further - (1:3:5) times then inc row once again. *- (49:51:53) sts.*

All sizes again

Work a further 6 (5:10:8) rows straight.

Shape sleeve top

Cast off 2 (2:3:4) sts at beg of next 2 rows. *43 (45:45:45) sts.*

Dec I st at each end of next 7 (7:5:3) rows, on 4 (5:7:9) foll alt rows, then on foll 5 rows. *11 sts.*

Cast off 2 sts at beg of next 2 rows. *7 sts.*

Cast off remaining 7 sts.

BUTTONHOLE BAND

With RS facing, using 3.25mm needles and holding two ends of D together, pick up and k73 (76:78:81) sts up right front edge.

Work 2 rows in G-st as set on back.

Buttonhole row (WS): K4, sl I wyif, take yarn back, (leave yarn in back until directed otherwise), [sl I, pass slipped st over previous slipped st] 3 times (3 sts cast off), place the last st back on left hand needle, turn and wyib the cable cast on method, cast 3 sts onto left hand needle, cast on I more st but before putting st on left needle bring yarn between 2 sts and to the front, turn, k1, pass final cast on st

over the st you have just worked, k2, [k9 (9:10:10), sl 1 wyif,
take yarn back, (leave yarn in back until directed otherwise),
[sl 1, pass slipped st over previous slipped st] 3 times (3 sts
cast off), place the last st back on left hand needle, turn and
wyib using the cable cast on method, cast 3 sts onto left
hand needle, cast on 1 more st but before putting st on left
needle bring yarn between 2 sts and to the front, turn, k1,
pass final cast st over the st you have just worked, k2] twice,
k to end. *3 buttonholes made.*
Work a further 3 rows in G-st.
Cast off knitwise.

BUTTON BAND

With RS facing, using 3.25mm needles and holding two ends
of D together, pick up and k73 (76:78:81) sts down left
front edge.
Work 6 rows in G-st as set on Back.
Cast off knitwise.

COLLAR

Join shoulder seams.
With RS facing, using 3.25mm needles, holding a single
strand of D, beg at side edge of buttonhole band, pick up and
k23 (23:24:25) sts up right front neck edge, 30 (30:32:32) sts
from back neck and 23 (23:24:25) sts down left front neck
edge to end of button border. *76 (76:80:82) sts.*
Next row: Knit.
Next row: K4, p to last 4 sts, k4.
Rep last 2 rows until collar measures 5 (5:6:6)cm /
2 (2:2½:2½)in, ending with a RS row.
Work 5 rows in G-st as set on Back.
Cast off knitwise.

MAKING UP

Join side and sleeve seams. Set in sleeves. Sew on buttons.

Button Cuff Bootees

Materials

YARN

Rowan Pure Wool DK
1 (1:1) x 50g ball in cloud 058
also shown in hyacinth 026 and
clay 048

NEEDLES

Pair of 3.75mm (UK 9/US 5) knitting
needles
1 extra needle in a similar size to work the
3-needle cast off

EXTRAS

Stitch holder (optional)
2 small buttons

MEASUREMENTS

To fit age

	0-6 months	6-9 months	9-12 months

TENSION

24 sts and 40 rows to 10cm (4in) square over G-st using 3.75mm needles, or size to obtain correct tension.

NOTES

These garter stitch bootees are made in one piece, from top to bottom, with just a small back seam to sew.

ABBREVIATIONS

See page 78

PATTERN BEGINS (make 2 alike)

Note: Where only one number is given this applies to all sizes.

CUFF

Cast on 16 sts and working in G-st throughout, knit an even number of rows for 13 (14:16.5)cm / 5 (5½:6½)in.

Next row: Cast off 8 sts knitwise, k to end. *8 sts.*

Knit 10 rows.

Buttonhole row: K2, sl1 wyif, take yarn back, (leave yarn in back until directed otherwise), [sl1, pass slipped st over previous slipped st] 3 times (3 sts cast off), place the last st back on left hand needle, turn and wyib using the cable cast on method, cast 3 sts onto left hand needle, cast on 1 more st but before putting st on left needle bring yarn between 2 sts and to the front, turn, k1 and pass the final cast on st over this st, k2. *8 sts on needle.*

Knit 2 rows.

Cast off knitwise.

FOOT

With RS facing, pick up and k30 (34:38) sts evenly along the shorter of the side edges.

Knit 8 (8:10) rows.

Shape toes

Next row: K20 (22:24) sts, turn and continue on these sts only.

Next row: K10, turn and continue on these 10 sts only leaving remaining 20 (22:24) sts on hold.

Knit 14 (16:15) rows.

Next row: With RS facing, pick up and k7 (8:9) sts evenly along the side of instep, k10 (12:14) sts on needle.

Next row: K17 (20:23), M1, k10, M1, pick up and k7 (8:9) sts along other side of instep, k remaining 10 (12:14) sts. *46 (52:58) sts.*

Knit 6 rows.

Shaping sole

Next row: K3, k2tog, k14 (17:20), k2tog, k4, k2tog, k14 (17:20), k2tog, k3. *42 (48:54) sts.*

Next row: Knit.

Next row: K3, k2tog, k12 (15:18), k2tog, k4, k2tog, k12

(15:18), k2tog, k3. *38 (44:50) sts.*

Next row: Knit.

Next row: K3, k2tog, k10 (13:16), k2tog, k4, k2tog, k10 (13:16), k2tog, k3. *34 (40:46) sts.*

Next row: K17 (20:23) to halfway point of row. With WS facing, fold in half and using third needle, work a 3-needle cast-off.

MAKING UP

Using mattress stitch, join back seam.

Turn the cuff down. Sew on buttons securely.

PomPom Hat

Materials

YARN

Rowan Pure Wool 4 ply

A: 1 × 50g ball

B: 1 × 50g ball

Version 1: (A) Shale 402 and (B) Eau de Nil 450

Version 2: (A) Snow 412 and (B) Shell 468

NEEDLES

Pair of 3.25mm (UK 10/US 3) knitting needles

EXTRAS

1 small pom pom maker (optional)

MEASUREMENTS

To fit age					
	0-6 months	6-9 months	9-12 months	12-18 months	
Actual measurements					
Circumference					
	34	35	37	39	cm
	13½	13¾	14¼	15	in

TENSION

27 sts and 42 rows to 10cm (4in) over twisted G-st using 3.25mm needles, or size to obtain correct tension.

ABBREVIATIONS

See page 78

PATTERN BEGINS

Using A, cast on 87 (90:95:98) sts.

Row I (RS): K18 (17:15:19), [kfb, k16 (13:12:9)] 3 (4:5:6) times, kfb, k to end. *91 (95:101:105) sts.*

Next row: K each st tbl to end.

Last row sets twisted G-st.

Continue in twisted G-st as set until work measures 9 (10:11:12)cm / 3½ (4:4¼:4¾)in from cast-on edge, ending with a WS row.

Shape Crown

Next row: K1 (2:1:2)tbl, [k2togtbl, k11 (11:12:12)tbl,] 6 times, k2togtbl, k10 (13:14:17)tbl. *84 (88:94:98) sts.*

Work 5 rows in twisted G-st.

Next row: K1 (2:1:2)tbl, [k2togtbl, k10 (10:11:11)tbl] 6 times, k2togtbl, k9 (12:13:16)tbl. *77 (81:87:91) sts.*

Work 5 rows in twisted G-st.

Next row: K1 (2:1:2)tbl, [k2togtbl, k9 (9:10:10)tbl] 6 times, k2togtbl, k8 (11:12:15)tbl. *70 (74:80:84) sts.*

Work 5 rows in twisted G-st.

Next row: K1 (2:1:2)tbl, [k2togtbl, k8 (8:9:9)tbl] 6 times, k2togtbl, k7 (10:11:14)tbl. *63 (67:73:77) sts.*

Work 5 rows in twisted G-st.

Next row: K1 (2:1:2)tbl, [k2togtbl, k7 (7:8:8)tbl] 6 times, k2togtbl, k6 (9:10:13)tbl. *56 (60:66:70) sts.*

Work 3 rows in twisted G-st.

Next row: K1 (2:1:2)tbl, [k2togtbl, k6 (6:7:7)tbl] 6 times, k2togtbl, k5 (8:9:12)tbl. *49 (53:59:63) sts.*

Work 3 rows in twisted G-st.

Next row: K1 (2:1:2)tbl, [k2togtbl, k5 (5:6:6)tbl] 6 times, k2togtbl, k4 (7:8:11)tbl. *42 (46:52:56) sts.*

Work 3 rows in twisted G-st.

Next row: K1 (2:1:2)tbl, [k2togtbl, k4 (4:5:5)tbl] 6 times, k2togtbl, k3 (6:7:10)tbl. *35 (39:45:49) sts.*

Work 1 row in twisted G-st.

Next row: K1 (2:1:2)tbl, [k2togtbl, k3 (3:4:4)tbl] 6 times, k2togtbl, k2 (5:6:9)tbl. *28 (32:38:42) sts.*

Work 1 row in twisted G-st.

3rd and 4th sizes only

Next row: K- (-:1:2)tbl, [k2togtbl, k- (-:3:3)tbl] 6 times, k2togtbl, k- (-:5:8)tbl. *- (-:31:35) sts.*

Work 1 row.

All sizes again

Next row: K1 (2:1:2)tbl, [k2togtbl, k2tbl] 6 times, k2togtbl, k1 (4:4:7)tbl. *21 (25:24:28) sts.*

Work 1 row.

Next row: K1 (2:1:2)tbl, [k2togtbl, k1tbl] 6 times, k2togtbl, k0 (3:3:6)tbl. *14 (18:17:21) sts.*

Next row: [K2togtbl] 7 (9:8:10) times, k0 (0:1:1). *7 (9:9:10) sts.*

Break yarn and thread through remaining sts. Fasten off.

MAKING UP

Join back seam using mattress stitch. Weave in all loose ends.

POMPOM

Using B, make a pompom. I find the easiest way is with a pompom maker. After tying off, leave enough yarn to stitch it securely to the top of the hat.

HELPFUL TECHNIQUE

icord bind off

The i-cord bind off is just great for when a regular bind off just doesnt feel or look right. I have used this within my patterns to create a lovely eding to the piece, keeping it neat and tidy. This is a technique which may seem a little confusing at first, but as soon as you remeber the process its a great way to finish your work.

ONE: Cast on 3 stitches to the left needle.

TWO: Knit the first two stitches (that you just cast on) and slip the third.

THREE: Knit 1 (from your last row).

FOUR: Pass the slipped stitch over.

FIVE: Replace the 3 stitches back on your left needle.

Repeat the four steps until you have cast off all of your stitches. Working with a contrasting colour helps you keep track of stitches, but you can

also use the same colour you worked the rest of your pattern in. It may feel like you are working far more stitches in this bind off, but once you memorise the method it will go quite quickly and the end results are certainly worth it.

ABBREVIATIONS

alt	Alternate
beg	Beginning
cm	Centimetres
dec	Decrease(d)
DPNs	Double-pointed needles
foll(s)	Following/Follows
g	Gram(s)
G-st	Garter stitch (knit every row)
in	Inch(es)
inc	Increase(d)
k	Knit
k2tog	Knit 2 stitches together (decrease 1)
k2togtbl	Knit 2 stitches together through the back loop (decrease 1)
kfb	Knit into the front then back of stitch (increase 1)
M1	Make 1 stitch: Picking up loop between last and next stitch and knit through the back loop
patt	Pattern
patt2tog	Work 2 stitches together to maintain pattern (decrease 1)
PM	Place marker
p	Purl
p2tog	Purl 2 stitches together (decrease 1)
pfb	Purl into the front then back of stitch (increase1)
pwise	Purlwise
Rep	Repeat
RS	Right side of work
sl	Slip
skp	Slip 1 stitch, knit the next stitch, pass slipped stitch over (decrease 1)
spp	Slip 1 stitch, purl the next stitch, pass slipped stitch over (decrease 1)
SM	Slip marker
st(s)	Stitch(es)
St-st	Stocking stitch (stockinette); Worked flat: knit on RS, purl on WS Worked in the round: knit every round
tbl	Through the back loop
w&t	Wrap and turn
wyib	With yarn in back
wyif	With yarn in front
WS	Wrong side of work
yf	Yarn forward
yo	Yarn over needle
yrn	Yarn round needle

STOCKISTS

AUSTRALIA: Australian Country Spinners, Pty Ltd, Level 7, 409 St. Kilda Road, Melbourne Vic 3004.
Tel: 03 9380 3888   Fax: 03 9820 0989   Email: customerservice@auspinners.com.au

AUSTRIA: Coats Harlander Ges.m.b.H.., Autokaderstraße 29, 1210 Wien, Austria
Tel: 00800 26 27 28 00   Fax: (00) 49 7644 802-133
Email: coats.harlander@coats.com   Web: www.coatscrafts.at

BELGIUM: Coats N.V., c/o Coats GmbH Kaiserstr.1 79341 Kenzingen Germany
Tel: 0032 (0) 800 77 89 2   Fax: 00 49 7644 802 133   Email: sales.coatsninove@coats.com
Web: www.coatscrafts.be

BULGARIA: Coats Bulgaria, 7 Magnaurska Shkola Str., BG-1784 Sofia, Bulgaria
Tel: (+359 2) 976 77 41   Fax: (+359 2) 976 77 20   Email: officebg@coats.com
Web: www.coatsbulgaria.bg

CANADA: Westminster Fibers, 10 Roybridge Gate, Suite 200, Vaughan, Ontario L4H 3M8
Tel: (800) 263-2354   Fax: 905-856-6184   Email: info@westminsterfibers.com

CHINA: Coats Shanghai Ltd, No 9 Building , Baosheng Road, Songjiang Industrial Zone, Shanghai.
Tel: (86- 21) 13816681825   Fax: (86-21) 57743733-326   Email: victor.li@coats.com

CYPRUS: Coats Bulgaria, 7 Magnaurska Shkola Str., BG-1784 Sofia, Bulgaria
Tel: +359 2) 976 77 41   Fax: (+359 2) 976 77 20   Email: officebg@coats.com
Web: www.coatscrafts.com.cy

CZECH REPUBLIC: Coats Czecho s.r.o.Staré Mesto 246 569 32
Tel: (420) 461616633   Email: galanterie@coats.com

ESTONIA: Coats Eesti AS, Ampri tee 9/4, 74001 Viimsi Harjumaa
Tel: +372 630 6250   Fax: +372 630 6260   Email: info@coats.ee   Web: www.coatscrafts.co.ee

DENMARK: Carl J. Permin A/S Egegaardsvej 28 DK-2610 Rødovre
Tel: (45) 36 72 12 00   E-mail: permin@permin.dk

FINLAND: Coats Opti Crafts Oy, Huhtimontie 6 04200 KERAVA
Tel: (358) 9 274871   Email: coatsopti.sales@coats.com   www.coatscrafts.fi

FRANCE: Coats France, c/o Coats GmbH, Kaiserstr.1, 79341 Kenzingen, Germany
Tel: (0) 0810 06 00 02   Email: artsdufil@coats.com   Web: www.coatscrafts.fr

GERMANY: Coats GmbH, Kaiserstr. 1, 79341 Kenzingen, Germany
Tel: 0049 7644 802 222   Email: kenzingen.vertrieb@coats.com   Fax: 0049 7644 802 300
Web: www.coatsgmbh.de

GREECE: Coats Bulgaria, 7 Magnaurska Shkola Str., BG-1784 Sofia, Bulgaria
Tel: (+359 2) 976 77 41   Fax: (+359 2) 976 77 20   Email: officebg@coats.com
Web: www.coatscrafts.gr

HOLLAND: Coats B.V., c/o Coats GmbH, Kaiserstr.1 79341 Kenzingen, Germany
Tel: 0031 (0) 800 02 26 6488   Fax: 00 49 7644 802 133   Email: sales.coatsninove@coats.com
Web: www.coatscrafts.be

HONG KONG: East Unity Company Ltd, Unit B2, 7/F., Block B, Kailey Industrial Centre, 12 Fung Yip Street, Chai Wan
Tel: (852)2869 7110   Email: eastunityco@yahoo.com.hk

ICELAND: Storkurinn, Laugavegi 59, 101 Reykjavik
Tel: (354) 551 8258   Email: storkurinn@simnet.is

ITALY: Coats Cucirini srl, Viale Sarca no 223, 20126 Milano
Tel: 02636151   Fax: 0266111701

KOREA: Coats Korea Co. Ltd, 5F Eyeon B/D, 935-40 Bangbae-Dong, 137-060
Tel: (82) 2 521 6262   Fax: (82) 2 521 5181   Email: rozenpark@coats.com

LATVIA: Coats Latvija SIA, Mukusalas str. 41 b, Riga LV-1004
Tel: +371 67 625173   Fax: +371 67 892758   Email: info.latvia@coats.com
Web: www.coatscrafts.lv

LEBANON: y.knot, Saifi Village, Mkhalissiya Street 162, Beirut
Tel: (961) 1 992211   Fax: (961) 1 315553   Email: y.knot@cyberia.net.lb

LITHUANIA & RUSSIA: Coats Lietuva UAB, A. Juozapaviciaus str. 6/2, LT-09310 Vilnius
Tel: +370 527 30971   Fax: +370 527 2305   Email: info@coats.lt   Web: www.coatscrafts.lt

LUXEMBOURG: Coats N.V., c/o Coats GmbH, Kaiserstr.1, 79341 Kenzingen, Germany
Tel: 00 49 7644 802 222   Fax: 00 49 7644 802 133   Email: sales.coatsninove@coats.com
Web: www.coatscrafts.be

MALTA: John Gregory Ltd, 8 Ta'Xbiex Sea Front, Msida MSD 1512, Malta
Tel: +356 2133 0202   Fax: +356 2134 4745   Email: raygreg@onvol.net

MEXICO: Estambres Crochet SA de CV, Aaron Saenz 1891-7, PO Box SANTAMARIA, 64650 MONTERREY
TEL +52 (81) 8335-3870

NEW ZEALAND: ACS New Zealand, P.O. Box 76199, Northwood, Christchurch New Zealand
Tel: 64 3 323 6665   Fax: 64 3 323 6660   Email: lynn@impactmg.co.nz

NORWAY: Carl J. Permin A/S Egegaardsvej 28 DK-2610 Rødovre
Tel: (45) 36 72 12 00   E-mail: permin@permin.dk

PORTUGAL: Coats & Clark, Quinta de Cravel, Apartado 444, 4431-968 Portugal
Tel: 00 351 223 770700

SINGAPORE: Golden Dragon Store, 101 Upper Cross Street #02-51, People's Park Centre, Singapore 058357
Tel: (65) 6 5358454   Fax: (65) 6 2216278   Email: gdscraft@hotmail.com

SLOVAKIA: Coats s.r.o.Kopcianska 94851 01 Bratislava
Tel: (421) 263532314   Email: galanteria@coats.com

SOUTH AFRICA: Arthur Bales LTD, 62 4th Avenue, Linden 2195
Tel: (27) 11 888 2401   Fax: (27) 11 782 6137   Email: arthurb@new.co.za

SPAIN: Coats Fabra SAU, Avda Meridiana 350, pta 13, 08027 Barcelona
Tel: (34) 932908400   Fax: 932908409   Email: atencion.clientes@coats.com

SWEDEN: Carl J. Permin A/S Egegaardsvej 28 DK-2610 Rødovre
Tel: (45) 36 72 12 00   E-mail: permin@permin.dk

SWITZERLAND: Coats Stroppel AG, Stroppelstrasse 20, 5417 Untersiggenthal, Switzerland
Tel: 00800 2627 2800   Fax: 0049 7644 802 133   Email: coats.stroppel@coats.com
Web: www.coatscrafts.ch

TAIWAN: Cactus Quality Co Ltd, 7FL-2, No. 140, Sec.2 Roosevelt Rd, Taipei, 10084 Taiwan, R.O.C.
Tel: 00886-2-23656527   Fax: 886-2-23656503   Email: cqcl@ms17.hinet.net

THAILAND: Global Wide Trading, 10 Lad Prao Soi 88, Bangkok 10310
Tel: 00 662 933 9019   Fax: 00 662 933 9110   Email: global.wide@yahoo.com

U.S.A.: Westminster Fibers, 8 Shelter Drive, Greer, South Carolina, 29650
Tel: (800) 445-9276   Fax: 864-879-9432   Email: info@westminsterfibers.com

U.K: Rowan, Green Lane Mill, Holmfirth, West Yorkshire, England HD9 2DX
Tel: +44 (0) 1484 681881   Fax: +44 (0) 1484 687920   Email: ccuk.sales@coats.com
Web: www.knitrowan.com

Publishers Acknowledgements;

The publishers would like to thank Kate Buller, David MacLeod and all the team at Rowan for all of their support . To all the team behind the scenes, and to Sarah Hatton for her assistance while working on this title. To our baby model AJ and his mother Fran for being just superb on the shoot. Finally a big thank-you to all of our active followers on Social Media and our Blog, who keep us filled with ideas and support our titles.

Team Quail ~ @QuailBooks

For new release information and up to date information about our titles follow us;

www.quailpublishing.co.uk
@QuailBooks